Study Guide

Essentials of Statistics for the Behavioral Sciences

SIXTH EDITION

Frederick J Gravetter

State University College at Brockport

Larry B. Wallnau

State University College at Brockport

Prepared by

Frederick J Gravetter

State University College at Brockport

WADSWORTH
CENGAGE Learning™

Australia • Brazil • Japan • Korea • Mexico • Singapore • Spain • United Kingdom • United States

WADSWORTH
CENGAGE Learning™

Study Guide, Essentials of Statistics for the Behavioral Sciences, Sixth Edition
Frederick J Gravetter, Larry B. Wallnau

For product information and technology assistance, contact us at
Cengage Learning Customer & Sales Support, 1-800-354-9706

For permission to use material from this text or product, submit all requests online at **www.cengage.com/permissions**
Further permissions questions can be emailed to
permissionrequest@cengage.com

ISBN-13: 978-0-495-38529-5

ISBN-10: 0-495-38529-8

Wadsworth
10 Davis Drive
Belmont, CA 94002-3098
USA

Cengage Learning is a leading provider of customized learning solutions with office locations around the globe, including Singapore, the United Kingdom, Australia, Mexico, Brazil, and Japan. Locate your local office at: **international.cengage.com/region**

Cengage Learning products are represented in Canada by Nelson Education, Ltd.

For your course and learning solutions, visit **academic.cengage.com**

Purchase any of our products at your local college store or at our preferred online store **www.ichapters.com**

Printed in Canada
2 3 4 5 6 7 11 10 09 08

CONTENTS

How to Use
This Study Guide

As the title indicates, the purpose of a Study Guide is to provide you with a guide for studying. In general, studying involves revisiting and reviewing material that you have already seen in class and in the textbook. Notice that we have used the word "review," as in "a second look." The textbook is written to provide an introduction to statistical concepts, and includes all the explanations and examples necessary to present new ideas that students are seeing for the first time. This *Study Guide*, on the other hand, is written to provide a second look at material that is already somewhat familiar. That is, the Study Guide is intended as a "review" that condenses, summarizes, and highlights the textbook. Thus, the Study Guide is a supplement to the textbook, not a replacement for the textbook, and we strongly suggest that you work in the Study Guide only after you have read and studied the corresponding section in the textbook.

Each chapter in the Study Guide corresponds to a chapter in the textbook, and each Study Guide chapter is divided into seven major sections. The following paragraphs provide an overview of these sections and some suggestions for how they should be used.

Chapter Summary We begin with a big-picture overview of the chapter contents. The intent is to provide a relatively concise summary of the general content of the chapter and to identify most of the major points. This is the kind of thing that your mother wanted to know when she asked, "What did you learn in school today?" If you understand the big picture, then all the details, terminology, and formulas will be much easier to learn. Keep in mind, however, that the summary does not include all of the individual topics that are covered in the chapter. You will need to read the complete chapter and work some of the problems before you will pick up all the details.

Learning Objectives. Next we provide a list of goals that should be achieved upon completion of studying a text chapter. These objectives usually are task-oriented, pointing to specific things you should know how to do or how to explain. If you lack confidence in meeting any of these objectives, you should return to the appropriate section(s) of the text for further study.

New Terms And Concepts This section consists of a list of important terms and concepts that appeared in the text. You should identify or define these terms, and explain how closely-related terms are interrelated. Return to the text to check your answers.

New Formulas A list of formulas that were introduced in the text is provided. For each formula, you should test yourself in the following way:
   1) Identify each symbol and term in the formula.
   2) Make a list of the computational steps that are indicated by the formula.
   3) Describe when each formula is used and explain why it is used or what it is computing.
   4) Most importantly, you should realize that each formula is simply a concise, mathematical expression of a concept or procedure. If you can explain the concept or procedure in words, then it is usually very easy to translate the words into mathematical symbols and recreate the formula. Thus, we encourage you to understand concepts rather than memorize formulas.

Step-By-Step This section presents a typical problem (or problems) from the chapter and provides a demonstration of the step-by-step procedures for solving the problem.

Hints and Cautions. In this section, we provide advice on the typical mistakes students make, and the difficulties they commonly have with the chapter material.

Self-Test. In this section we present a series of questions and problems that provide a general review of the chapter. As much as possible, the problems consist of simple sets of numbers so that you can solve them with minimal calculation. Work through the Self-Test carefully, and remember that your mistakes will tell you what areas need additional study. Incidentally, the **Answers to the Self-Test** are given at the end of each Study Guide chapter. For problems with numerical answers, do not fret about slight differences between your answer and ours. A little rounding error is to be expected.

STUDY HINTS

It seems appropriate for a study guide to have a few suggestions to help you study. The following are some hints that have proved useful for our own students.

1. You will learn (and remember) much more if you study for short periods several times a week, rather than concentrating all your studying into one long session. For example, it is far more effective to study for one-half hour every night than to spend a single three and one-half hour session once a week.

2. Do some work before class. Read the appropriate sections in the textbook before your instructor presents the material in class. Although you may not completely understand what you read, you will have a general idea of the topic which will make the lecture easier to follow. Also, you can identify items that are particularly confusing and then be sure that these items are clarified in class.

3. Pay attention and think during class. Although this may sound like obvious advice, many students spend their class time frantically taking notes rather than listening and understanding what is being said. For example, it usually is not necessary to copy down every sample problem that your instructor works in class. There are plenty of example problems in your textbook and in this study guide - you probably do not need one more in your notebook. Just put down your pencil and pay attention. Be sure that you understand what is being done, and try to anticipate the next step in the problem.

4. Test yourself regularly. Do not wait until the end of the chapter or the end of the week to check your knowledge. After each lecture, work some of the end-of-chapter problems, do the learning checks, and be sure you can define key terms. If you are having trouble, get your questions answered immediately (re-read the text, go to your instructor, ask questions in class). Do not let yourself fall behind.

5. Don't kid yourself. Many students sit in class watching the instructor solve problems, and think to themselves, "This looks easy, I understand it." Do you really? Can you do the problem all by yourself? Many students use the examples in the textbook as a guide for working assigned problems. They begin the problem, get stuck, then check the example to see what to do next. A minute later they are stuck again, so they take another peek at the example in the text. Eventually, the problem is finished and the students think that they understand how to solve problems. Although there is nothing wrong with using examples as models for solving problems, you should try working a problem with your book closed to determine whether you can complete it on your own.

PREPARING FOR EXAMS

1.   Perhaps the best way to get ready for an exam is to make up your own exam. This is particularly effective if you have a friend in the class so you can both make up exams and then exchange them. Constructing your own exam forces you to identify the important points in the material, and it makes you think about how exam questions might be phrased. It is very satisfying to open a statistics exam and find some questions that you wrote yourself the day before.

2.   Many students suffer from "exam anxiety" which causes them to freeze up and forget everything during exams. One way to help avoid the problem is for you to take charge of your own time during an exam.

    a. Don't spend a lot of time working on one problem that you really don't understand (especially if it is a 1-point true/false question). Just move on to the rest of the exam - you can come back later, if you have time.

    b. Remember that you do not have to finish the exam questions in the order they are presented. When you get your exam, go immediately to the problems you understand best. This will build some confidence and make you better prepared for the remainder of the exam.

Probably the best way to reduce exam anxiety is to practice taking exams. Make up your own exam (select problems from the book and study guide) or have a friend make up an exam. Then try to duplicate the general conditions of an exam. If you are not allowed to use your book during exams, then put it away during practice. Give yourself a time limit. If you have an old alarm clock, set it in front of you so that you can hear the ticking and watch the time slip away. You might even try sitting in front of a mirror so that every time you look up there is someone watching you.

Finally, remember that very few miracles happen during exams. The work on your exam is usually a good reflection of your studying and understanding. Most students walk into an exam with a very good idea of how well they will do. Be honest with yourself. If you are well prepared, you will do well on the exam, and there is no reason to panic. If you are not prepared, then exam anxiety probably is not your problem.

CHAPTER 1

INTRODUCTION TO STATISTICS

CHAPTER SUMMARY

The goals of Chapter 1 are:
1. To introduce the basic terminology that will be used in statistics.
2. To explain how statistical techniques fit into the general process of scientific research.
3. To introduce some of the notation that will be used throughout the rest of the book.

Terminology

A **variable** is a characteristic or condition that can change or take on different values. Most research begins with a general question about the relationship between two variables for a specific group of individuals. The entire group of individuals is called the **population**. For example, a researcher may be interested in the relation between class size (variable 1) and academic performance (variable 2) for the population of third-grade children. Usually populations are so large that a researcher cannot examine the entire group. Therefore, a **sample** is selected to represent the population in a research study. The goal is to use the results obtained from the sample to help answer questions about the population.

Variables can be classified as discrete or continuous. **Discrete variables** (such as class size) consist of indivisible categories, and **continuous variables** (such as time or weight) are infinitely divisible into whatever units a researcher may choose. For example, time can be measured to the nearest minute, second, half-second, etc.) To define the units for a continuous variable, a researcher must use **real limits** which are boundaries located exactly half-way between adjacent categories.

To establish relationships between variables, researchers must observe the variables and record their observations. This requires that the variables be **measured**. The process of measuring a variable requires a set of categories called a **scale of measurement** and a process that classifies each individual into one category. Four types of measurement scales are as follows:

a. A **nominal scale** is an unordered set of categories identified only by name. Nominal measurements only permit you to determine whether two individuals are the same or different.

b. An **ordinal scale** is an ordered set of categories. Ordinal measurements tell you the direction of difference between two individuals.
c. An **interval scale** is an ordered series of equal-sized categories. Interval measurements identify the direction and magnitude of a difference.
d. A **ratio scale** is an interval scale where a value of zero indicates none of the variable. Ratio measurements identify the direction and magnitude of differences and allow ratio comparisons of measurements.

Two broad categories of research studies are experiments and correlational studies. The goal of a **correlational** study is to determine whether there is a relationship between two variables and to describe the relationship. A **correlational** study simply observes the two variables as they exist naturally, and the data consist of two scores (two measurements) for each individual. The goal of an **experiment** is to demonstrate a cause-and-effect relationship between two variables; that is, to show that changing the value of one variable causes changes to occur in a second variable. In an **experiment**, the researcher manipulates one variable by changing its value to create two or more treatment conditions. A second variable is observed and measured to obtain scores for a group of individuals in each of the treatment conditions. The measurements are then compared to see if there are differences between treatment conditions. All other variables are controlled to prevent them from influencing the results. In an experiment, the manipulated variable is called the **independent variable** and the observed variable is the **dependent variable**.

Other types of research studies, know as **non-experimental**, have the same structure as experiments because they also compare groups of scores. However, these studies do not use a manipulated variable to differentiate the groups. Instead, the variable that differentiates the groups is usually a pre-existing participant variable (such as male/female) or a time variable (such as before/after). Because these studies do not use the manipulation and control of true experiments, they cannot demonstrate cause and effect relationships. As a result, they are similar to correlational research because they simply demonstrate and describe relationships between variables.

Statistics in Science

The measurements obtained in a research study are called the **data**. The goal of statistics is to help researchers organize and interpret the data. Statistical techniques are classified into two broad categories: descriptive and inferential. **Descriptive statistics** are methods for organizing and summarizing data. For example, tables or graphs are used to organize data, and descriptive values such as the average score are used to summarize data. A descriptive value for a population is called a **parameter** and a descriptive value for a sample is called a **statistic**. **Inferential statistics** are methods for using sample data to make general conclusions (inferences) about populations. Because a sample is typically only a part of the whole population, sample data provide only limited information about the population. As a result, sample statistics are generally imperfect representatives of the corresponding population parameters. The discrepancy between a sample statistic and its population parameter is called **sampling error**. The concept of sampling error is demonstrated in Figure 1.2 in the textbook. Defining and measuring sampling error is a large part of inferential statistics.

Notation

The individual measurements or scores obtained for a research participant will be identified by the letter X (or X and Y if there are multiple scores for each individual). The number of scores in a data set will be identified by N for a population or n for a sample.

Summing a set of values is a common operation in statistics and has its own notation. The Greek letter sigma, Σ, will be used to stand for "the sum of." For example, ΣX identifies the sum of the scores. To use and interpret summation notation, you must follow the basic **order of operations** required for all mathematical calculation.

1. All calculations within parentheses are done first.
2. Squaring or raising to other exponents is done second.
3. Multiplying, and dividing are done third, and should be completed in order from left to right.
4. Summation with the Σ notation is done next.
5. Any additional adding and subtracting is done last and should be completed in order from left to right.

For example, to compute $\Sigma X + 3$, you sum the X values, then add 3.
To compute $\Sigma(X + 3)^2$, you add 3 to each X (inside parentheses), then square the resulting values, then sum the squared numbers.

LEARNING OBJECTIVES

1. You should be familiar with the terminology and special notation of statistical methods.

2. You should understand the purpose of statistics: When, how, and why they are used.

3. You should understand summation notation and be able to use this notation to represent mathematical operations and to compute specified sums.

NEW TERMS AND CONCEPTS

The following terms were introduced in Chapter 1. You should be able to define or describe each term and, where appropriate, describe how each term is related to other terms in the list.

population	The entire group of individuals that a researcher wishes to study.
sample	A group selected from a population to participate in a research study.
statistic	A characteristic that describes a sample.
parameter	A characteristic that describes a population.
sampling error	The discrepancy between a statistic and a parameter.
descriptive statistics	Techniques that organize and summarize a set of data.
inferential statistics	Techniques that use sample data to draw general conclusions about populations.
variable	A characteristic that can change or take on different values.
constant	A characteristic that does not change.
raw score	An original, unaltered measurement.
dependent variable	In an experiment, the variable that is observed for changes. (the scores)
independent variable	In an experiment, the variable that is manipulated by the researcher. (the treatment conditions)
correlational method	A research method that simply observes two existing variables to determine the nature of their relationship.

experimental method	A research method that manipulates one variable, observes a second variable for changes, and controls all other variables. The goal is to establish a cause-and-effect relationship.
control condition	A condition where the treatment is not administered.
experimental condition	A condition where the treatment is administered.
hypothetical construct	A characteristic or mechanism that is assumed to exist but cannot be observed or measured directly.
operational definition	A procedure for measuring and defining a construct.
nominal scale	A measurement scale where the categories are differentiated only by qualitative names.
ordinal scale	A measurement scale consisting of a series of ordered categories.
interval scale	An ordinal scale where all the categories are intervals with exactly the same width.
ratio scale	An interval scale where a value of zero corresponds to none.
discrete variable	A variable that exists in indivisible units.
continuous variable	A variable that can be divided into smaller units without limit.
real limits	The boundaries separating the intervals that define the scores for a continuous variable.
Σ	Summation sign - the sum of.
N and n	The number of scores in a population or a sample.
X	A score.

STEP BY STEP

Summation Notation: In statistical calculations you constantly will be required to add a set of values to find a specific total. We will use algebraic expressions to represent the values being added (for example, X = score), and we will use the Greek letter sigma (Σ) to signify the process of summation. Occasionally, you simply will be adding a set of scores, ΣX. More often, you will be doing some initial computation and then adding the results. For example, we will routinely need to square each score and then find the sum of the squared values, ΣX^2. The following step-by-step process should help you understand summation notation and use it correctly to find appropriate totals.

Step 1: A mathematical expression that includes summation notation (Σ) can be viewed as a set of step-by-step instructions. Your job is to identify the different steps and then perform them in the proper order. To accomplish this, you must follow the order of operations presented earlier (page 3).

Step 2: Set up a computational table listing the original X values in the first column. As you perform each step in the order of operations, you will create a new column showing the results of that step.

Suppose your task is to find $\Sigma(X + 3)$. The first step according to these instructions is to add three points to each X values (inside parentheses). Start a new column headed with (X + 3), and list each value you obtain as you add three points to the original X scores.

X	(X + 3)
4	7
8	11
2	5
6	9

Note: Occasionally you will need more than one column to get to the final term you want. To compute $\Sigma(X + 3)^2$, for example, begin with the X column, then add a column of (X + 3) values, and then add a third column that squares each of the (X + 3) values. Thus, each column represents a step in the computations.

X	(X + 3)	$(X + 3)^2$
4	7	49
8	11	121
2	5	25
6	9	81

Step 3: When you reach the point where the next step in the order of operations is the summation, simply add all the values in the appropriate column.

Using the same numbers that we used in Step 2, you find $\Sigma(X + 3)$ by simply adding the values in the $(X + 3)$ column.

$$\Sigma(X + 3) = 7 + 11 + 5 + 9 = 32$$

To find $\Sigma(X + 3)^2$ you add the values in the $(X + 3)^2$ column.

$$\Sigma(X + 3)^2 = 49 + 121 + 25 + 81 = 276.$$

HINTS AND CAUTIONS

1.   Many students confuse the independent variable and the dependent variable in an experiment. It may help you to differentiate these terms if you visualize the results (the data) from a typical experiment.

		Treatment 1	Treatment 2
Independent Variable Manipulated to create Treatment Conditions	$\longrightarrow$	12	24
		10	21
Dependent Variable		14	29
The scores measured	$\longrightarrow$	16	23
In each treatment		11	22

The goal is to determine whether the scores depend on the treatments. In this example, the scores in Treatment 2 appear to be higher than the scores in Treatment 1.

2.   There are three specific sums that are used repeatedly in statistics calculations. You should know the notation and computations for each of the following:
a. ΣX^2 First square each score, then add the squared values.
b. $(\Sigma X)^2$ First sum the scores, then square the total.
c. $\Sigma(X - C)^2$ First subtract the constant C from each score, then square each of the resulting values. Finally, add the squared numbers.

SELF TEST

True/False Questions

1. A summary value, usually numerical, that describes a population is called a parameter.

2. A researcher is interested in the vocabulary skills of 3-year-old children. For this researcher, the entire set of 3-year-old children would be the *population*.

3. A researcher interested in human memory selects a group of 30 students to participate in a research study. The group of 30 students would be considered a *population*.

4. In statistical notation, a lower-case letter n is used to identify the number of scores in a population.

5. The average salary for a sample of n = 20 doctors would be an example of a parameter.

6. The correlational research method requires manipulation and control of variables to establish a relationship.

7. Determining the favorite color for each child in a pre-school class would be an example of measurement on a nominal scale.

8. A research report states that rats that were housed in a high humidity environment ate less food that rats housed in a low humidity environment. For this report, the dependent variable is the amount of food each rat eats.

9. To compute $\Sigma X + 3$, you first add 3 points to each score and then find the sum of the resulting values.

10. For any set of scores, $\Sigma X^2 = (\Sigma X)^2$.

1. Although research questions usually concern a _____, the actual research is typically conducted with a _____.
    a. sample, statistic
    b. population, parameter
    c. sample, population
    d. population, sample

2. A researcher is interested in the eating behavior of rats and selects a group of 25 rats to be tested in a research study. The group of 25 rats is a _____.
    a. sample
    b. statistic
    c. population
    d. parameter

3. A researcher is interested in the effect of St. Johns Wort on memory. A group of 25 college students is selected to participate in a research study. The average memory score obtained for the 25 students is a _____.
    a. sample
    b. statistic
    c. population
    d. parameter

4. The relationship between a parameter and a statistic is the same as the relationship between a population and a(n) _____.
    a. variable
    b. constant
    c. score
    d. sample

5. A researcher wants to examine the relationship between sleeping habits and grade point average for college students. A group of 100 students is selected and each student is asked to report the average number of hours he/she sleeps each night and his/her grade point average. What research method is being used in this study?
    a. experimental method
    b. correlational method
    c. non-experimental method comparing two groups
    d. none of the above

6. A researcher observed that preschool children placed in a red room showed more aggressive behavior than children placed in a blue room. For this study, what is the independent variable?
    a. preschool children
    b. color of the room
    c. amount of aggression
    d. the children's play

7. In a study evaluating the effectiveness of a new medication designed to control high blood pressure, one sample of individuals is given the medicine and a second sample is given an inactive placebo. Blood pressure is measured for each individual. For this study, what is the dependent variable?
    a. the medication
    b. the placebo
    c. blood pressure
    d. the individuals given the medication

8. To determine the size of the difference between two measurements, a researcher must use a(n) _____ scale of measurement.
    a. nominal
    b. ordinal or interval
    c. interval or ratio
    d. ratio

9. Determining a person's occupation would involve measurement on a(n) _____ scale of measurement.
    a. nominal
    b. ordinal
    c. interval
    d. ratio

10. A variable that has an infinite number of possible values between any two specific measurements is called a(n) _____ variable.
    a. independent
    b. dependent
    c. discrete
    d. continuous

11. Which of the following is an example of a discrete variable?
    a. height
    b. reaction time
    c. number of brothers and/or sisters
    d. age

12. What is the first step to be performed when computing $\Sigma (X - 2)^2$?
    a. square each value
    b. subtract 2 points from each score
    c. sum the values
    d. compute $2^2 = 4$

13. For the following scores, what is $(\Sigma X)^2$?   Scores: 2, 0, 4, 2
    a. 16
    b. 24
    c. 64
    d. $(24)^2 = 576$

14. For the following scores, what is $\Sigma X + 1$?   Scores: 2, 0, 4, 2
    a. 9
    b. 11
    c. 12
    d. 36

15. You are instructed to add 1 point to each score, then square the resulting values, and then find the sum of the squared numbers. In summation notation, this set of operations would be expressed as
    a. $(\Sigma X + 1)^2$
    b. $\Sigma(X + 1)^2$
    c. $\Sigma(X^2 + 1)$
    d. $\Sigma X^2 + 1$

Other Questions

1. Describe the relationships between a *sample*, a *population*, a *statistic* and a *parameter*.

2. What are the basic characteristics of an experiment that differentiate this method from other types of research?

3. Compute each value requested for the following set of scores.

X	
1	ΣX
0	ΣX^2
5	$(\Sigma X)^2$
2	N

4. Compute each value requested for the following set of scores.

X	
0	$\Sigma X + 1$
6	$\Sigma(X + 1)$
4	$\Sigma(X + 1)^2$
3	

5. Use summation notation to express each of the following calculations.
   a.   Square each score, then find the sum of the squared scores.
   b.   Add the scores, then square the total.
   c.   Add 3 points to each score, then find the sum of the resulting values.
   d.   Find the sum of the scores, then add 10 points to the total.
   e.   Subtract 1 point from each score, then square each of the resulting values.
         Next, find the sum of the squared numbers. Finally, add 5 points to this sum.

ANSWERS TO SELF TEST

True/False Answers

1.   True.
2.   True.
3.   False. The 30 students would be a sample.
4.   False. The lower-case n indicates a sample.
5.   False. The average for a sample is a statistic.
6.   False. The experimental method requires manipulation and control.
7.   True
8.   True.
9.   False. You sum the scores, then add 3 points to the sum.
10.   False. The two expressions require different steps and produce different
       answers.

Multiple-Choice Answers

1. d Populations are usually too large to study so researchers use samples.
2. a The group selected from the population to participate in the study is called the sample.
3. b A characteristic that describes a sample is called a statistic.
4. d A parameter describes a population and a statistic describes a sample.
5. b The correlational method simply measures two variables for each participant.
6. b The independent variable is manipulated by the researcher.
7. c The dependent variable is the score measured for each individual.
8. c An interval or ratio scale is needed to measure distance.
9. a Occupations are simply named categories.
10. d A continuous variable is infinitely divisible.
11. c Only whole numbers are possible with no intermediate values.
12. b Operations inside parentheses are done first.
13. c Sum the scores, then square the sum.
14. a Sum the scores, then add 1 to the sum.
15. b Adding 1 point is done in parentheses, then square, then add.

Other Answers

1. A population is the entire group of individuals that you are interested in studying. A sample is a group selected from the population to participate in the research study. A parameter is a characteristic, usually a numerical value, of a population. A statistic is a characteristic of a sample.

2. The goal of an experiment is to establish a cause-and-effect relationship between two variables. To accomplish this goal, an experiment has two distinguishing features. First, the researcher manipulates one variable (the independent variable) to create the different treatment conditions that will be compared. The dependent variable is the score that is measured inside each treatment condition. The second feature of an experiment is that all other variables are controlled so that they cannot influence the independent variable or the dependent variable.

3. $\Sigma X = 8$, $\Sigma X^2 = 30$, $(\Sigma X)^2 = 64$, $N = 4$

4. $\Sigma X + 1 = 13 + 1 = 14$
   $\Sigma(X + 1) = 1 + 7 + 5 + 4 = 17$
   $\Sigma(X + 1)^2 = 1 + 49 + 25 + 16 = 91$

5. a. ΣX^2
   b. $(\Sigma X)^2$
   c. $\Sigma(X + 3)$
   d. $\Sigma X + 10$
   e. $\Sigma(X - 1)^2 + 5$

CHAPTER 2

FRENQUENCY DISTRIBUTIONS

CHAPTER SUMMARY

The goals of Chapter 2 are:
1. To introduce the concept of a frequency distribution as a descriptive statistical technique.
2. To describe how a frequency distribution can be presented in a regular or grouped table.
3. To describe how a frequency distribution can be presented in a graph.

Frequency Distributions

       After collecting data, the first task for a researcher is to organize and simplify the data so that it is possible to get a general overview of the results. This is the goal of descriptive statistical techniques. One method for simplifying and organizing data is to construct a frequency distribution. A **frequency distribution** is an organized tabulation showing exactly how many individuals are located in each category on the scale of measurement. A frequency distribution presents an organized picture of the entire set of scores, and it shows where each individual is located relative to others in the distribution.

Frequency Distribution Tables

       A **frequency distribution table** consists of at least two columns - one listing categories on the scale of measurement (X) and another for frequency (f). In the X column, values are listed from the highest to lowest, without skipping any. For the frequency column, tallies are determined for each value (how often each X value occurs in the data set). These tallies are the frequencies for each X value. The sum of the frequencies should equal N. A third column can be used for the proportion (p) for each category: $p = f/N$. The sum of the p column should equal 1.00. Finally, a fourth column can display the percentage of the distribution corresponding to each X value. The percentage is found by multiplying p by 100. The sum of the percentage column is 100%.

When a frequency distribution table lists all of the individual categories (X values) it is called a **regular frequency distribution**. Sometimes, however, a set of scores covers a wide range of values. In these situations, a list of all the X values would be quite long - too long to be a "simple" presentation of the data. To remedy this situation, a **grouped frequency distribution** table is used. In a grouped table, the X column lists groups of scores, called **class intervals**, rather than individual values. These intervals all have the same width, usually a simple number such as 2, 5, 10, and so on. Each interval begins with a value that is a multiple of the interval width. The interval width is selected so that the table will have approximately ten intervals.

Frequency Distributions Graphs

In a **frequency distribution graph**, the score categories (X values) are listed on the X axis and the frequencies are listed on the Y axis. When the score categories consist of numerical scores from an interval or ratio scale, the graph should be either a histogram or a polygon. In a **histogram**, a bar is centered above each score (or class interval) so that the height of the bar corresponds to the frequency and the width extends to the real limits, so that adjacent bars touch. In a **polygon**, a dot is centered above each score so that the height of the dot corresponds to the frequency. The dots are then connected by straight lines. An additional line is drawn at each end to bring the graph back to a zero frequency.

When the score categories (X values) are measurements from a nominal or an ordinal scale, the graph should be a bar graph. A **bar graph** is just like a histogram except that gaps or spaces are left between adjacent bars.

If it is possible to count the number of scores in a population, then the population distribution can be presented in a histogram, polygon, or bar graph. However, many populations are so large that it is impossible to know the exact number of individuals (frequency) for any specific category. In these situations, population distributions can be shown using **relative frequency** instead of the absolute number of individuals for each category. If the scores in the population are measured on an interval or ratio scale, it is customary to present the distribution as a **smooth curve** rather than a jagged histogram or polygon. The smooth curve emphasizes the fact that the distribution is not showing the exact frequency for each category.

Frequency distribution graphs are useful because they show the entire set of scores. At a glance, you can determine the highest score, the lowest score, and where the scores are centered. The graph also shows whether the scores are clustered together or scattered over a wide range. Finally, a graph shows the **shape** of the distribution. A distribution is **symmetrical** if the left side of the graph is (roughly) a mirror image of the right side. One example of a symmetrical distribution is the bell-shaped normal distribution. On the other hand, distributions are **skewed** when scores pile up on one side of the distribution, leaving a "tail" of a few extreme values on the other side. In a

positively skewed distribution, the scores tend to pile up on the left side of the distribution with the tail tapering off to the right. In a **negatively skewed** distribution, the scores tend to pile up on the right side and the tail points to the left.

LEARNING OBJECTIVES

1. Know how to organize data into regular or grouped frequency distribution tables.

2. Be able to construct graphs, including bar graphs, histograms, and polygons.

3. Be able to describe the shape of a distribution portrayed in a frequency distribution graph.

NEW TERMS AND CONCEPTS

The following terms were introduced in this chapter. You should be able to define or describe each term and, where appropriate, describe how each term is related to other terms in the list.

frequency distribution	A tabulation of the number of individuals in each category on the scale of measurement.
grouped frequency distribution	A frequency distribution where scores are grouped into intervals rather than listed as individual values.
class interval	A group of scores in a grouped frequency distribution.
upper real limit	The boundary that separates an interval from the next higher interval.
lower real limit	The boundary that separates an interval from the next lower interval.
apparent limits	The score values that appear as the lowest score and the highest score in an interval.

histogram	A graph showing a bar above each score or interval so that the height of the bar corresponds to the frequency and width extends to the real limits.
polygon	A graph consisting of a line that connects a series of dots. A dot is placed above each score or interval so that the height of the dot corresponds to the frequency.
bar graph	A graph showing a bar above each score or interval so that the height of the bar corresponds to the frequency. A space is left between adjacent bars.
relative frequency	The proportion of the total distribution rather than the absolute frequency. Used for population distributions for which the absolute number of individuals is not known for each category.
symmetrical distribution	A distribution where the left-hand side is a mirror image of the right-hand side.
positively skewed distribution	A distribution where the scores pile up on the left side and taper off to the right.
negatively skewed distribution	A distribution where the scores pile up on the right side and taper off to the left.
tail(s) of a distribution	A section on either side of a distribution where the frequency tapers down toward zero as the X values become more extreme.

NEW FORMULAS

proportion $= p = f/N$

percentage $= p(100) = (f/N)(100)$

STEP BY STEP

Constructing a Frequency Distribution Table: The goal of a frequency distribution table is to take an entire set of scores and simplify and organize them into a form that allows a researcher to see at a glance the entire distribution. Suppose, for example, that an instructor gave a personality questionnaire measuring self-esteem to an entire class of psychology students. The questionnaire classifies each individual into one of five categories indicating different levels of self esteem: 1 = high self-esteem and 5 = low self-esteem.

The results for the class are as follows:

4, 4, 3, 3, 5, 4, 2, 1, 1, 3
4, 4, 5, 2, 3, 3, 4, 3, 3, 2
1, 4, 5, 3, 4, 4, 5, 2, 4, 1
3, 3, 2, 2, 4, 5, 1, 5, 3, 4

Step 1: In the first column of the table, list the categories that make up the scale of measurement starting with the highest score at the top and listing every possible X value down to the lowest score. The column heading should be "X" to indicate that this is the scale of X values.

X
5
4
3
2
1

Step 2: In a second column, headed by "f" for frequency, list the number of individuals who have each score. For example, six people have scores of $X = 5$, so you place a 6 in the f column beside the X value 5. Continue for each score (category) on the scale of measurement.

X	f
5	6
4	12
3	11
2	6
1	5

The result is a basic frequency distribution table. The table can be expanded by adding columns for proportion or percentage.

<u>Retrieving Scores from a Frequency Distribution Table</u>: Although a frequency distribution table provides a concise overview of an entire set of data, it is a condensed version of the actual data and for some students the table can obscure the details of the individual scores. For example, in the table that we have just constructed, the 40 individual scores have been condensed into a table that shows only 10 numerical values (five X's and five frequencies).   For some purposes, it is easier to transform a frequency distribution table back into a complete set of scores before you begin any statistical calculations with the data. We will use the table we have already constructed to demonstrate the process of recovering individual scores from a frequency distribution table.

Step 1: Find the number of individual scores (N): The frequency column (f) of the table shows the number of individuals located in each category on the scale of measurement. For this example, six individuals had scores of $X = 5$, twelve individuals had scores of $X = 4$, and so on. To determine the total number of individuals in the group, you simply add the frequencies.

$N = \Sigma f = 6 + 12 + 11 + 6 + 5 = 40$

Step 2: List the complete set of individual scores: Again, the table shows that six individual had scores of $X = 5$, twelve individuals had $X = 4$, and so on. These scores can be listed individually as follows:

5, 5, 5, 5, 5, 5	six fives
4, 4, 4, 4, 4, 4, 4, 4, 4, 4, 4, 4	twelve fours
3, 3, 3, 3, 3, 3, 3, 3, 3, 3, 3	eleven threes
2, 2, 2, 2, 2, 2	six twos
1, 1, 1, 1, 1	five ones

With the complete set of $N = 40$ scores listed in this way, it is easy to perform computations based on individual scores. For example, to find ΣX you would add the 40 values ($\Sigma X = 128$).

HINTS AND CAUTIONS

1. When making the list of intervals for a grouped frequency distribution table, some people find it easier to begin the list with the lowest interval and work up to the highest. Fewer mistakes will be made.

2. When interpreting a frequency distribution table, be sure to use both columns, X and f, to get a complete list of the entire set of scores. Remember, the X column does not list all the scores, it simply shows the scale of measurement.

SELF TEST

True/False Questions

1. The purpose for constructing a frequency distribution table is to get an organized view of the entire set of scores.

2. When listing scores in a frequency distribution table, you should not skip any scores, even if one has a frequency of zero.

3. In a frequency distribution table, the ΣX may be obtained by simply adding the values in the column labeled X.

4. If the lowest score is $X = 15$ and the highest score is $X = 44$, then a grouped frequency distribution table should be used.

5. By convention, a grouped frequency distribution table is structured so that the number of intervals (the number of rows in the table) is a simple number such as 2, or 5, or 10.

6. In a grouped frequency distribution table, one class interval is identified as 15-19. This interval has a width of four points.

7. In a frequency distribution graph, the scores (X values) are listed on the vertical axis.

8. A professor records the academic major for each student in a class. If these data are presented in a frequency distribution graph, the graph should *not* be a polygon.

9. Bar graphs are used for data that are measured on a nominal or an ordinal scale.

10.   When the scores pile up on the right-hand side of a distribution and taper off to the left, then the distribution is positively skewed.

Multiple-Choice Questions

Questions 1 through 3 concern the following table.

X	f
5	1
4	2
3	4
2	1
1	2

1. For these data, N = _____.
   a. 10
   b. 15
   c. 29
   d. cannot be determined from the table

2. How many individuals had a score of X = 2?
   a. 1
   b. 2
   c. 3
   d. 4

3. For these data, ΣX is _____.
   a. 10
   b. 15
   c. 29
   d. cannot be determined from the table

4. A set of scores ranges from a high of X = 67 to a low of X = 23. If these scores are organized in a grouped frequency distribution table with an interval width of 5 points, then roughly how many intervals will be needed?
   a. 13-14
   b. around 9
   c. 44
   d. 45

5. Which types of graphs are used for data from an interval scale?
    a. histograms and bar graphs
    b. polygons and bar graphs
    c. histograms and polygons
    d. histograms, bar graphs, and polygons

6. A distribution of scores is being organized in a grouped frequency distribution table with an interval width of 2 points. If the lowest score in the distribution is $X = 41$, then the bottom interval in the table should be _____.
    a. 40-42
    b. 41-43
    c. 40-41
    d. 41-42

7. A set of scores ranges from a high of $X = 96$ to a low of $X = 11$. If these scores are placed in a grouped frequency distribution table, the best value for the interval width is _____.
    a. 2 points
    b. 5 points
    c. 9 points
    d. 10 points

Questions 8 and 9 refer to the following table showing a frequency distribution of exam scores.

X	f
70-74	3
65-69	4
60-64	8
55-59	2
50-54	1
45-49	1

8. This is a grouped frequency distribution table where the scores have been grouped into class intervals using an interval width of _____.
    a. 4 points
    b. 5 points
    c. 9 points
    d. 10 points

9. The lowest score on the exam is _____.
   a. X = 45
   b. X = 49
   c. X = 47.5
   d. cannot be determined from the information given

Questions 10-12 refer to the following figure.

10. What type of frequency distribution graph is shown in the figure on the left side?
    a. histogram
    b. polygon
    c. bar graph
    d. cumulative graph

11. What type of frequency distribution graph is shown in the figure on the right side?
    a. histogram
    b. polygon
    c. bar graph
    d. cumulative graph

12. What is the best description for the shape of this distribution?
    a. normal
    b. symmetrical
    c. positively skewed
    d. negatively skewed

13. If a distribution of scores is shown in a bar graph, you know that the scores were measured on a _____ scale of measurement.
- a. nominal or ordinal
- b. ordinal or interval
- c. interval or ratio
- d. discrete or continuous

14. The normal distribution is an example of
- a. a histogram showing data from a sample
- b. a polygon showing data from a sample
- c. a bar graph showing data from a population
- d. a smooth curve showing data from a population

15. What shape would you expect for the distribution of scores from a very hard exam for a large class of students?
- a. positively skewed
- b. negatively skewed
- c. symmetrical
- d. normal

Other Questions

1. Simplifying and organizing data is the goal of descriptive statistics. One descriptive technique is to organize a set of scores in a frequency distribution. Define a frequency distribution and explain how it simplifies and organizes data.

2. Occasionally it is necessary to group scores into class intervals and construct a grouped frequency distribution.
- a. Explain when it is necessary to use a grouped table (as opposed to a regular table).
- b. Outline the guidelines for constructing a grouped frequency table.

3. A frequency distribution graph can be either a histogram, a bar graph, or a polygon. Define each of these graphs and identify the circumstances where each is used.

4. For the following set of scores:
   5, 4, 2, 3, 4, 3, 6, 4, 2, 4, 2, 3, 5, 4, 3
   a. Construct a frequency distribution table including columns for frequency, proportion, and percentage.
   b. Draw a histogram showing the data.

ANSWERS TO SELF TEST

True/False Answers

1. True
2. True
3. False. To find ΣX you must consider the f values as well as the X values.
4. True
5. False. A grouped table should have about 10 intervals.
6. False. The interval width is 5 points.
7. False. The X values are listed on the horizontal axis.
8. True
9. True
10. False. The tail is pointing toward the negative side.

Multiple-Choice Answers

1. a N is determined by Σf.
2. a The number of individuals is shown in the f column beside each X.
3. c Remember to include the frequencies. You must add all 10 scores.
4. b The scores cover a range of 45 points.
5. c Interval scale data can be shown in a histogram or a polygon.
6. c The bottom score is a multiple of the width.
7. d The range is 86 points.
8. b Each interval is 5 points wide.
9. d There is one individual in the 45-49 interval but the exact score is unknown.
10. a A histogram consists of bars with no gaps between them.
11. b A polygon consists of series of dots connected by lines.
12. d The tail points toward the left (negative side).
13. a A bar graph is used for scores from a nominal or ordinal scale.
14. d The normal distribution is a smooth curve used for population data.
15. a Most students would have low score (left-hand side of the distribution).

Other Answers

1. A frequency distribution shows the number of individuals located in each category on the scale of measurement.

2. a. A grouped frequency distribution table is needed when the range of scores is large, causing a frequency distribution table to have too many entries in the X column.
    b. In a grouped frequency distribution table the guidelines are:
        1. You should strive for approximately 10 rows in the table.
        2. Interval widths of 2, 5, 10, 20, 50, and 100 should be used. (Select the interval width that satisfies guideline 1.)
        3. The first (lowest) value of each interval should be a multiple of the interval width.
        4. List all intervals without skipping any. The top interval should contain the highest observed X value and the bottom interval should contain the lowest observed X value.

3. In a histogram there is a bar above each score (or interval) showing the frequency. Adjacent bars are touching. A histogram is used with interval or ratio data. A bar graph is similar to a histogram except that there are spaces between the bars and the bar graph is used with nominal or ordinal data. In a polygon, the frequency is indicated by a dot above each score (or interval), and the dots are connected with straight lines. A polygon is used with interval or ratio data.

4. a.

X	f	p	%
6	1	.07	7%
5	2	.13	13%
4	5	.33	33%
3	4	.27	27%
2	3	.20	20%

b.

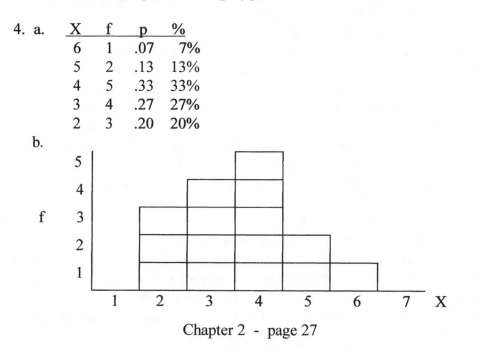

CHAPTER 3

CENTRAL TENDENCY

CHAPTER SUMMARY

The goals of Chapter 3 are:
1. To introduce central tendency as a descriptive statistical procedure.
2. To introduce the three basic measures of central tendency: the mean, the median, and the mode.
3. To describe how measures of central tendency are related to the shape of the distribution.
4. To describe how central tendency is presented in research reports, including presentation in graphs.

Central Tendency

In general terms, **central tendency** is a statistical measure that determines a single value that accurately describes the center of the distribution and represents the entire distribution of scores. The goal of central tendency is to identify the single value that is the best representative for the entire set of data.

By identifying the "average score," central tendency allows researchers to summarize or condense a large set of data into a single value. Thus, central tendency serves as a descriptive statistic because it allows researchers to describe or present a set of data in a very simplified, concise form. For example, the reading ability for an entire third-grade class can be summarized by the average reading score. In addition, it is possible to compare two (or more) sets of data by simply comparing the average score (central tendency) for one set versus the average score for another set. For example, a report may summarize research results by stating that the patients who received medication had an average cholesterol level 50 points lower than patients without medication.

The Mean, the Median, and the Mode

It is essential that central tendency be determined by an objective and well-defined procedure so that others will understand exactly how the "average" value was obtained and can duplicate the process. However, no single procedure always produces a good, representative value. Therefore, researchers have developed three commonly used techniques for measuring central tendency: the mean, the median, and the mode.

The Mean The mean is the most commonly used measure of central tendency. Computation of the mean requires scores that are numerical values measured on an interval or ratio scale. The mean is obtained by computing the sum, or total, for the entire set of scores, then dividing this sum by the number of scores.

For sample data the mean is: $\quad M = \dfrac{\Sigma X}{n}$

For population data the mean is: $\quad \mu = \dfrac{\Sigma X}{N}$

Conceptually, the mean can also be defined as:
1. The mean is the amount that each individual receives when the total (ΣX) is divided equally among all N individuals.
2. The mean is the balance point of the distribution because the sum of the distances below the mean is exactly equal to the sum of the distances above the mean.

Because the calculation of the mean involves every score in the distribution, changing the value of any score will change the value of the mean. Also, modifying a distribution by discarding scores or by adding new scores will usually change the value of the mean. To determine how the mean will be affected for any specific situation you must consider: 1) how the number of scores is affected, and 2) how the sum of the scores is affected. For example, adding a new score to a distribution will increase the number of scores by 1, and will increase ΣX by the value of the new score.

If a constant value is added to every score in a distribution, then the same constant value is added to the mean. Also, if every score is multiplied by a constant value, then the mean is also multiplied by the same constant value.

Although the mean is the most commonly used measure of central tendency, there are situations where the mean does not provide a good, representative value, and there are situations where you cannot compute a mean at all. When a distribution contains a few extreme scores (or is very skewed), the mean will be pulled toward the extremes (displaced toward the tail). In this case, the mean will not provide a "central" value. With data from a nominal scale it is impossible to compute a mean, and when data are measured on an ordinal scale (ranks), it is usually inappropriate to compute a mean. Thus, the mean does not always work as a measure of central tendency and it is necessary to have alternative procedures available.

The Median If the scores in a distribution are listed in order from smallest to largest, the median is defined as the midpoint of the list. The median divides the scores so that 50% of the scores in the distribution have values that are equal to or less than the median. Computation of the median requires scores that can be placed in rank order (smallest to largest) and are measured on an ordinal, interval, or ratio scale. Usually, the median can be found by a simple counting procedure:
1. With an odd number of scores, list the values in order, and the median is the middle score in the list.
2. With an even number of scores, list the values in order, and the median is half-way between the middle two scores.

If the scores correspond to measurements of a continuous variable, it is possible to find the median by first placing the scores in a frequency distribution histogram with each score represented by a box in the graph. Then, draw a vertical line through the distribution so that exactly half the boxes are on each side of the line. The median is defined by the location of the line.

One advantage of the median is that it is relatively unaffected by extreme scores. Thus, the median tends to stay in the "center" of the distribution even when there are a few extreme scores or when the distribution is very skewed. In these situations, the median serves as a good alternative to the mean.

The Mode The mode is defined as the most frequently occurring category or score in the distribution. In a frequency distribution graph, the mode is the category or score corresponding to the peak or high point of the distribution. The mode can be determined for data measured on any scale of measurement: nominal, ordinal, interval, or ratio.

It is possible for a distribution to have more than one mode. For example, a frequency distribution graph may have two peaks, with a mode at each peak. Such a distribution is called **bimodal**. (Note that a distribution can have only one mean and only one median.) In addition, the term "mode" is often used to describe a peak in a distribution that is not really the highest point. Thus, a distribution may have a *major mode* at the highest peak and a *minor mode* at a secondary peak in a different location.

The primary value of the mode is that it is the only measure of central tendency that can be used for data measured on a nominal scale. In addition, the mode often is used as a supplemental measure of central tendency that is reported along with the mean or the median.

Central Tendency and the Shape of the Distribution

Because the mean, the median, and the mode are all measuring central tendency, the three measures are often systematically related to each other. In a symmetrical distribution, for example, the mean and median will always be equal. If a symmetrical distribution has only one mode, the mode, mean, and median will all have the same value. In a skewed distribution, the mode will be located at the peak on one side and the mean usually will be displaced toward the tail on the other side. The median is usually located between the mean and the mode.

Reporting Central Tendency in Research Reports

In manuscripts and in published research reports, the sample mean is identified with the letter M. There is no standardized notation for reporting the median or the mode. In research situations where several means are obtained for different groups or for different treatment conditions, it is common to present all of the means in a single graph. The different groups or treatment conditions are listed along the horizontal axis and the means are displayed by a bar or a point above each of the groups. The height of the bar (or point) indicates the value of the mean for each group. Similar graphs are also used to show several medians in one display.

LEARNING OBJECTIVES

1. You should be able to define central tendency and you should understand the general purpose of obtaining a measure of central tendency.

2. You should be able to define and compute each of the three basic measures of central tendency for a set of data.

3. You should know how the mean is affected when a set of scores is modified. For example, what happens to the mean when a new score is added to an existing set, or when a score is removed, or when the value of a score is changed. In addition, you should know what happens to the mean when a constant value is added to every score in a distribution, or when every score is multiplied by a constant value.

4. You should know when each of the three measures of central tendency is used and you should understand the advantages and disadvantages of each.

5. You should know how the three measures of central tendency are related to each other for symmetrical distributions and for skewed distributions.

6. You should be able to draw and understand graphs showing the relationship between an independent variable and a dependent variable, where a measure of central tendency (usually the mean) is used to present the "average" score for the dependent variable.

NEW TERMS AND CONCEPTS

The following terms were introduced in this chapter. You should be able to define or describe each term and, where appropriate, describe how each term is related to other terms in the list.

central tendency	A statistical measures that identifies a single score (usually a central value) to serve as a representative for the entire group.
mean	The value obtained when the sum of the scores is divided by the number of scores.
median	The score that divides a distribution exactly in half.
mode (major and minor)	The score with the greatest frequency overall (major), or the greatest frequency within the set of neighboring scores (minor).
weighted mean	The average of two means, calculated so that each mean is weighted by the number of scores it represents.

NEW FORMULAS

$$\mu = \frac{\Sigma X}{N}$$

$$M = \frac{\Sigma X}{n}$$

STEP BY STEP

The Weighted Mean: Occasionally a researcher will find it necessary to combine two (or more) sets of data, or to add new scores to an existing set of data. Rather than starting from scratch to compute the mean for the new set of data, it is possible to compute the weighted mean. To find the new mean you need two pieces of information:

    1) How many scores are in the new data set?

    2) What is the sum of all the scores?

Remember, the mean is the sum of the scores divided by the number. We will use the following problem to demonstrate the calculation of the weighted mean.

    A researcher wants to combine the following three samples into a single group. Notice that sample 3 is actually a single score, $X = 4$. What is the mean for the combined group?

Sample 1	Sample 2	Sample 3
$n = 8$	$n = 5$	$n = 1$
$M = 12$	$M = 9$	$M = 4$

Step 1: To find n and ΣX for the combined group, the first step is to find n and ΣX for each of the individual samples. For example, sample 1 consists of $n = 8$ scores with a mean of $M = 12$. You can find ΣX for the scores by using the formula for the mean, and substituting the two values that you know,

$$M = \frac{\Sigma X}{n}$$

In this case,

$$12 = \frac{\Sigma X}{8}$$

Multiplying both sides of the equation by 8 gives,

$$8(12) = \Sigma X$$
$$96 = \Sigma X$$

Often this process is easier to understand if you put dollar-signs on the numbers and remember that the mean is the amount that each individual receives if the total is divided equally. For this example, we have a group of $n = 8$ people and, if the total amount is divided equally, each person will get \$12 (M). If the group puts all their money together (ΣX), how much will they have? Again the answer is $\Sigma X = \$96$.

Chapter 3 - page 33

Step 2:   Repeat the process in Step 1 for each individual data set. If the problem involves adding a single score to an existing data set, then you can treat the single score as a sample with n = 1 and X = M = ΣX.

For this example, Sample 2 has a n = 5 and ΣX = 45, and Sample 3 has n = 1 and ΣX = 4.

Step 3:   Once you have determined n and ΣX for each individual data set, then you simply add the individual n values to find the number of scores in the combined set. In the same way, you simply add the ΣX values to find the overall sum of the scores in the combined data set.   For this example,
   combined n = 8 + 5 + 1 = 14
   combined ΣX = 96 + 45 + 4 = 145

Step 4:   Finally you compute the mean for the combined group using the regular formula for M.

$$M \ = \ \Sigma X/n \ = \ \ 145/14 \ = \ \ 10.36$$

HINTS AND CAUTIONS

1.   One of the most common errors in computing central tendency occurs when students are attempting to find the mean for data in a frequency distribution table. You must remember that the frequency distribution table condenses a large set of scores into a concise, organized distribution; the table does not list each of the individual scores. One way of avoiding confusion is to transform the frequency distribution table back into the original list of scores. For example, the following frequency distribution table presents a distribution for which three individuals had scores of X = 5, one individual had X = 4, four individuals had X = 3, no one had X = 2, and two individuals had X = 1. When each of these scores is listed individually, it is much easier to see that N = 10 and ΣX = 33 for these data.

Frequency Distribution		Original X Values
X	f	
5	3	5
4	1	5
3	4	5
2	0	4
1	2	3
		3
		3
		3
		1
		1

2.   Many students incorrectly assume that the median corresponds to the midpoint of the range of scores. For example, it is tempting to say that the median for a 100-point test would be X = 50. Be careful! The correct interpretation is that the median divides the set of scores (or individuals) into two equal groups. On a 100-point   test, for example, the median could be X = 95, if the test was very easy and 50% of the class scored above 95. You must know where the individual scores are located before you can find the median.

Often it is easy to locate the median if you sketch a histogram of the frequency distribution. If each score is represented by a "block" in the graph, you can find the median by positioning a vertical line so that it divides the blocks into two equal piles.

SELF TEST

True/False Questions

1. Last summer I had three monthly phone bills of $20, $30, and $100. My mean monthly phone bill for the summer was $75.

2. Changing the value of a score in a distribution will always change the value of the mean.

3. After each score in a population is multiplied by 3, the mean is found to be $\mu = 90$. Based on this information, you can conclude that the original mean was $\mu = 30$.

4. A sample has a mean of M = 40. If a score of X = 55 is removed from the sample, then the sample mean will decrease.

5. On a 50 point exam Tom has a score of X = 23. This means that Tom scored below the median.

6. If one sample with a mean of M = 10 is combined with a second sample with a mean of M = 20, then the mean for the combined sample will be between 10 and 20.

7. A sample of n = 4 scores has a mean of M = 10. If a new score with a value of X = 5 is added to the sample, then the new sample will have a mean of 15.

8. In addition to having two modes, a bimodal distribution typically has two medians.

9. For a symmetrical distribution the mean is equal to the median.

10. A distribution with a mean $\mu = 50$ and a median of 70 probably is positively skewed.

Multiple-Choice Questions

1. For the population of scores shown in the frequency distribution table, the mean is
   a. $15/5 = 3$
   b. $15/12 = 1.25$
   c. $33/5 = 6.60$
   d. $33/12 = 2.75$

X	f
5	1
4	2
3	4
2	3
1	2

2. What is the mean for the following set of scores?   Scores: 1, 6, 10, 11
   a. 4
   b. 7
   c. 8
   d. 14

3. Which of the following is a property of the mean?
   a. Changing the value of a score will change the value of the mean.
   b. Adding a constant to each score will add the same constant to the mean.
   c. Multiplying each score by a constant will multiply the mean by the same constant.
   d. All 3 of the other choices are correct.

4. A sample of $n = 25$ scores has a mean of $M = 11$. If each score in the sample is multiplied by 6, the new mean would be _____.
   a. 11
   b. 6
   c. 66
   d. 150

5. A teacher gave a reading test to a class of 5th-grade students and computed the mean, median, and mode for the test scores. Which of the following statements *cannot* be an accurate description of the scores?
   a. No one had a score exactly equal to the mean.
   b. No one had a score exactly equal to the median.
   c. No one had a score exactly equal to the mode.
   d. All of the other options are false statements.

6. A professor records the academic major for each student in a class of n = 40. The best measure of central tendency for these data would be _____.
    a. the mean
    b. the median
    c. the mode
    d. Central tendency cannot be determined for these data.

7. A distribution of scores has a mean of $\mu = 50$. One new score is added to the distribution and the new mean is found to be $\mu = 52$. From this result you can conclude that the new score was _____.
    a. greater than 50
    b. less than 50
    c. equal to 52
    d. cannot answer from the information given

8. A sample of n = 20 scores has a mean of M = 55. After one score is removed from the sample, the mean for the remaining scores is found to be M = 51. From this information you can conclude that the removed score was _____.
    a. greater than 55
    b. less than 55
    c. equal to 55
    d. It is impossible to estimate the magnitude of the score from the information provided.

9. What is the median for the following set of scores?
        Scores: 1, 3, 9, 10, 22
    a. 6
    b. 9
    c. 9.5
    d. 11

10. A population with a mean of $\mu = 6$ has $\Sigma X = 42$. How many scores are in the population?
    a. N = 7
    b. N = 252
    c. N = 6/42 = 1/7
    d. cannot be determined from the information given

11. For a distribution of scores, the mean is equal to the median. This distribution is most likely to be _____.
   a. symmetrical
   b. positively skewed
   c. negatively skewed
   d. impossible to determine the shape

12. In a distribution of numerical scores with one or two extremely small values (very different from all the other scores), which measure of central tendency is more likely to produce a good representative value?
   a. the mean
   b. the median
   c. the mean and median would be equally good
   d. the mean and the median would both be distorted by the extreme scores

13. For a positively skewed distribution with $\mu = 30$, the median would have a value _____.
   a. equal to 30
   b. greater than 30
   c. less than 30
   d. cannot be determined from the information given

Questions 14 and 15 refer to the following figure

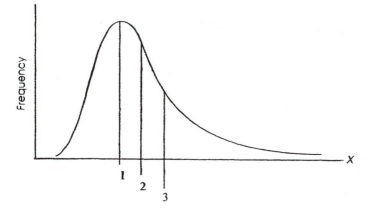

14. If the three locations marked in the figure correspond to the mean, the median, and the mode, which is the median?
   a. 1
   b. 2
   c. 3

15. If one of the scores in the extreme tail of the distribution were moved even farther to the right, which of the three measures of central tendency would also move farther to the right?

    a. 1

    b. 2

    c. 3

Other Questions

1. Explain the general purpose for obtaining a measure of central tendency.

2. A sample of $n = 4$ scores has a mean of $M = 8$.

    a. If a new score, $X = 3$, is added to the sample, what value will be obtained for the new sample mean?

    b. If one of the scores, $X = 5$, is removed from the original sample, what value would be obtained for the new sample mean?

    c. If one of the scores in the original sample is changed from $X = 10$ to $X = 18$, what value would be obtained for the new sample mean?

3. One sample has $n = 6$ and $M = 10$. A second sample has $n = 4$ scores with $M = 15$. If the two samples are combined, what is the value of the mean for the combined sample?

4. Compute the mean, median, and mode for the following set of scores.

    Scores: 5, 7, 5, 4, 3, 12, 9, 6, 6, 5, 7, 5, 6, 4

5. Compute the mean, median, and mode for the set of scores shown in the following frequency distribution table.

X	f
7	1
6	2
5	3
4	4
3	1
2	0
1	1

6. A researcher obtains the following results from an experiment comparing three treatment conditions:

    Treatment #1: $M = 12.7$

    Treatment #2: $M = 20.5$

    Treatment #3: $M = 8.4$

a. Assuming that the independent variable (the differences between treatments) is measured on a nominal scale, sketch a graph showing the experimental results.
b. Assuming that the independent variable is measured on an interval scale, sketch a graph showing the results.

ANSWERS TO SELF TEST

True/False Answers

1. False. The mean is $150/3 = 50$.
2. True
3. True
4. True
5. False. (not necessarily true). You need to know where the individual scores are located to determine the median.
6. True
7. False. The new score is relatively small compared to the others, and would cause the mean to decrease. The new mean is $45/5 = 9$.
8. False. There can never be two medians.
9. True
10. False. The smaller value for the mean indicates the tail is on the left side and the distribution is negatively skewed.

Multiple-Choice Answers

1. d You must use the frequencies as well as the X values.
2. b Add the four scores and divide by 4.
3. d All three are properties of the mean.
4. c Multiplying each score by a constant multiplies the mean by the same constant.
5. c The mode is the most commonly occurring score. There always will be scores located at the mode.
6. c The mode must be used for scores from a nominal scale.
7. a The mean increased, so the score must be greater than the old mean.
8. a Removing a large score will lower the mean.
9. b With an odd number of scores, the median is the middle value.
10. a The mean is $42/7 = 6$.
11. a In a symmetrical distribution, the mean = median, always.
12. b The mean may be displaced by the extreme scores.
13. c The mean is displaced toward the tail on the right-hand side.

14. b The mode is located at the peak and the mean is displaced toward the tail.

15. c Of the three measures, the mean is most affected by extreme scores.

Other Answers

1. The purpose of central tendency is to find a single value that best represents an entire distribution of scores.

2. a. With $n = 4$ and $M = 8$, the original sample has a total of $\Sigma X = 32$. Adding $X = 3$ produces $n = 5$ and $\Sigma X = 35$. The new mean is $35/5 = 7$.

    b. With $n = 4$ and $M = 8$, the original sample has a total of $\Sigma X = 32$. Taking away $X = 5$ leaves a sample with $n = 3$ scores and $\Sigma X = 27$. The new mean is $27/3 = 9$.

    c. Changing $X = 10$ to $X = 18$ adds 8 points to the total but does not change the number of scores. The new sample has $n = 4$ with $\Sigma X = 40$. The new mean is $40/4 = 10$.

3. The first sample has $n = 6$, $M = 10$, and $\Sigma X = 60$. The second sample has $n = 4$, $M = 15$, and $\Sigma X = 600$. When the samples are combined, the total number of score is $n = 10$ and the sum of the scores is $\Sigma X = 120$. The mean for the combined sample is $120/10 = 12$.

4. The mean is $84/14 = 6.00$. The median is $X = 5.5$, and the mode is $X = 5$.

5. The mean is $54/12 = 4.5$. The median is $X = 4.5$, and the Mode is $X = 4$.

6.   a.

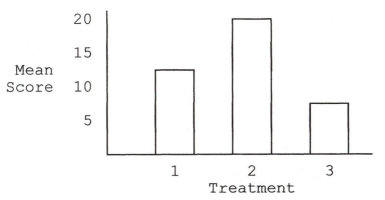

b. Use a histogram or a line graph (shown as follows).

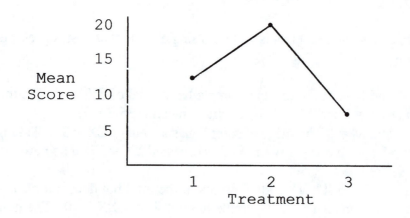

CHAPTER 4

VARIABILITY

CHAPTER SUMMARY

The goals of Chapter 4 are:
1. To introduce the concept of variability and to describe its importance as a descriptive measure and as a component of inferential statistics.
2. To introduce the basic techniques for measuring and describing variability: the range, the interquartile range, and the standard deviation/variance.
3. To demonstrate the properties of the standard deviation.
4. To demonstrate how the mean and standard deviation, working together, can provide a detailed description for a set of scores.

Variability

The goal for variability is to obtain a measure of how spread out the scores are in a distribution. A measure of variability usually accompanies a measure of central tendency as basic descriptive statistics for a set of scores. Central tendency describes the central point of the distribution, and variability describes how the scores are scattered around that central point. Together, central tendency and variability are the two primary values that are used to describe a distribution of scores.

Variability serves both as a descriptive measure and as an important component of most inferential statistics. As a descriptive statistic, variability measures the degree to which the scores are spread out or clustered together in a distribution. In the context of inferential statistics, variability provides a measure of how accurately any individual score or sample represents the entire population. When the population variability is small, all of the scores are clustered close together and any individual score or sample will necessarily provide a good representation of the entire set. On the other hand, when variability is large and scores are widely spread, it is easy for one or two extreme scores to give a distorted picture of the general population.

Measuring Variability: The Range, the Interquartile Range, and the Standard Deviation/Variance

Variability can be measured with the range, the interquartile range, or the standard deviation/variance. In each case, variability is determined by measuring *distance*. The **range** is the total distance covered by the distribution, from the highest score to the lowest score (using the upper and lower real limits of the range). The **interquartile range** is the distance covered by the middle 50% of the distribution (the difference between Q1 and Q3). **Standard deviation** measures the standard distance between a score and the mean. The calculation of standard deviation can be summarized as a four-step process:

1. Compute the deviation (distance from the mean) for each score.
2. Square each deviation.
3. Compute the mean of the squared deviations. For a population, this involves summing the squared deviations (sum of squares, SS) and then dividing by N. The resulting value is called the **variance** or *mean square* and measures the average squared distance from the mean.

    For samples, variance is computed by dividing the sum of the squared deviations (SS) by n - 1, rather than N. The value, n - 1, is know as degrees of freedom (df) and is used so that the sample variance will provide an unbiased estimate of the population variance.
4. Finally, take the square root of the variance to obtain the standard deviation.

Properties of the Standard Deviation

Because the standard deviation is probably the most commonly used measure of variability, it is important to understand how this descriptive measure is affected when a set of scores is transformed by either adding a constant or multiplying each score by a constant. If a constant is added to every score in a distribution, the standard deviation will *not* be changed. If you visualize the scores in a frequency distribution histogram, then adding a constant will move each score so that the entire distribution is shifted to a new location. The center of the distribution (the mean) changes, but the standard deviation remains the same. If each score is multiplied by a constant, the standard deviation will be multiplied by the same constant. Multiplying by a constant will multiply the distance between scores, and because the standard deviation is a measure of distance, it will also be multiplied.

The Mean and Standard Deviation as Descriptive Statistics

If you are given numerical values for the mean and the standard deviation, you should be able to construct a visual image (or a sketch)of the distribution of scores. For example, a set of scores with M = 80 and s = 10 will form a distribution that is centered at M = 80, with most of the scores located between 70 and 90 (within 10 points of the mean). As a general rule, about 70% of the scores will be within one standard deviation of the mean, and about 95% of the scores will be within a distance of two standard deviations of the mean.

LEARNING OBJECTIVES

1. Understand the measures of variability and be able to tell the difference between sets of scores with low versus high variability.

2. Know how to calculate SS (the sum of squared deviations) using either the computational or definitional formula.

3. Be able to calculate the population and sample variance and standard deviation, and understand the correction used in the formula for sample variance.

4. Be familiar with the characteristics of measures of variability, especially those for standard deviation.

NEW TERMS AND CONCEPTS

The following terms were introduced in this chapter. You should be able to define or describe each term and, where appropriate, describe how each term is related to other terms in the list.

variability	A measure of the degree to which the scores in a distribution are clustered together or spread apart.
range	The distance from the upper real limit of the highest score to the lower real limit of the lowest score; the total distance from the absolute highest point to the lowest point in the distribution.
first quartile	The score that separates the lowest 25% of a distribution from the highest 75%.
third quartile	The score that separates the lowest 75% of a distribution from the highest 25%.
interquartile range	The distance from the first quartile to the third quartile.
deviation score	The distance (and direction) from the mean to a specific score. Deviation $= X - \mu$.

population variance	The average squared distance from the mean; the mean of the squared deviations.
population standard deviation	The square root of the population variance; a measure of the standard distance from the mean.
sample variance	The sum of the squared deviations divided by $df = n - 1$. An unbiased estimate of the population variance.
sample standard deviation	The square root of the sample variance.
degrees of freedom	The number of scores in a sample that are independent and free to vary with no restriction. $df = n - 1$.
biased statistic	A statistic that, on average, consistently tends to overestimate (or underestimate) the corresponding population parameter.
unbiased statistic	A statistic that, on average, provides an accurate estimate of the corresponding population parameter. The sample mean and sample variance are unbiased statistics.

NEW FORMULAS

For a population:

$$SS = \Sigma(X - \mu)^2 \quad \text{or} \quad SS = \Sigma X^2 - \frac{(\Sigma X)^2}{N}$$

$$\sigma^2 = \frac{SS}{N} \qquad \sigma = \sqrt{\frac{SS}{N}}$$

For a sample:

$$SS = \Sigma(X - M)^2 \quad \text{or} \quad SS = \Sigma X^2 - \frac{(\Sigma X)^2}{n}$$

$$s^2 = \frac{SS}{n-1} \qquad s = \sqrt{\frac{SS}{n-1}} \qquad df = n-1$$

STEP BY STEP

SS, Variance, and Standard Deviation: The following set of data will be used to demonstrate the calculation of SS, variance, and standard deviation.
Scores: 5, 3, 2, 4, 1

Step 1:   Before you begin any calculation, simply look at the set of scores and make a preliminary estimate of the mean and standard deviation. For this set of data, it should be obvious that the mean is around 3, and most of the scores are within one or two points of the mean. Therefore, the standard deviation (standard distance from the mean) should be about 1 or 2.

Step 2:   Determine which formula you will use to compute SS. If you have a relatively small set of data and the mean is a whole number, then use the definitional formula. Otherwise, the computational formula is a better choice. For this example there are only 5 scores and the mean is equal to 3. The definitional formula would be fine for these scores.

Step 3:   Calculate SS. Note that it does not matter whether the set of scores is a sample or a population when you are computing SS. For this example, we will use formulas with population notation, but using sample notation would not change the result.

Definitional Formula: List each score in a column. In a second column put the deviation score for each X value. (Check that the deviations add to zero). In a third column list the squared deviation scores. Then simply add the values in the third column.

X	$(X - \mu)$	$(X - \mu)^2$
5	2	4
3	0	0
2	-1	1
4	1	1
1	-2	4
	0	10 = SS

Computational Formula: List each score in a column. In a second column list the squared value for each X. Then find the sum for each column. These are the two sums that are needed for the computational formula.

X	X^2	
5	25	
3	9	$\Sigma X = 15$
2	4	
4	16	$\Sigma X^2 = 55$
1	1	
15	55	

Then use the two sums in the computational formula to calculate SS.

$$SS = \Sigma X^2 - \frac{(\Sigma X)^2}{N} = 55 - (15)^2/5 = 55 - 45 = 10$$

Step 4: Now you must determine whether the set of scores is a sample or a population. With a population, you use N in the formulas for variance and standard deviation. With a sample, use n - 1.

For a Population

$$\sigma^2 = SS/N$$
$$= 10/5 = 2$$

$$\sigma = \sqrt{2} = 1.41$$

For a Sample

$$s^2 = SS/(n - 1)$$
$$= 10/4 = 2.5$$

$$s = \sqrt{2.5} = 1.58$$

HINTS AND CAUTIONS

1. Mistakes are commonly made in the computational formula for SS. Often, ΣX^2 is confused with $(\Sigma X)^2$. The ΣX^2 indicates that the X values are first squared, then summed. On the other hand, $(\Sigma X)^2$ requires that the X values are first added, then the sum is squared.

2. Remember, it is impossible to get a negative value for SS because, by definition, SS is the sum of the squared deviation scores. The squaring operation eliminates all of the negative signs.

3. The computational formula is usually easier to use than the definitional formula because the mean usually is not a whole number.

4. When computing a variance or a standard deviation, be sure to check whether you are computing the measure for a population or a sample. Remember, the sample variance uses n - 1 in the denominator so that it will provide an unbiased estimate of the population variance.

5. Note that you do not use n - 1 in the formula for sample SS. The value n - 1 is used to compute sample variance *after* you have calculated SS.

SELF TEST

True/False Questions

1. If the highest score in a distribution is $X = 8$ and the lowest score is $X = 2$, then the range is 6 points.

2. A deviation of –4 always indicates a score that is less than the mean.

3. When calculating SS, it is impossible to obtain a value less than zero unless a mistake is made.

4. If a sample has a variance of 16, then the sample standard deviation must be 4.

5. Subtracting 5 points from every score in a population will decrease the population variance.

6. The scores in a sample tend to be less variable than the scores in the population from which the sample was obtained.

7. A sample of n = 5 scores has SS = 20. The variance for this sample is 4.

8. A population of N = 5 scores has SS = 20. The variance for this population is 4.

9. For a specific set of scores, the value you obtain for SS will be the same whether the set of scores is a sample or a population.

10. In a distribution with μ = 40 and σ = 2, a score of X = 46 would be considered an extreme value (far out in the tail).

Multiple-Choice Questions

1. The value for the *range* is determined by _____.
    a. the two extreme scores (highest and lowest) in the distribution
    b. the extremely high scores in the distribution
    c. the middle scores in the distribution
    d. all of the scores in the distribution

2. The value for the standard deviation is determined by _____.
    a. the extreme scores (both high and low) in the distribution
    b. the extremely high scores in the distribution
    c. the middle scores in the distribution
    d. all of the scores in the distribution

3. What is the value of SS for the following set of scores? Scores: 5, 6, 1.
    a. 144
    b. 62
    c. 14
    d. None of the other choices is correct.

4. A sample of $n = 5$ scores has SS = 40. If the same five scores were a population, then the value obtained for the population SS would be _____.
    a. 40
    b. 5(40/4) = 50
    c. 4(40/5) = 32
    d. 5(40) = 200

5. Which of the following deviation scores corresponds to the score that is farthest away from the mean?
    a. 0
    b. 5
    c. –5
    d. –10

6. A population of $N = 10$ scores has $\mu = 50$ and SS = 200. For this population, what is the value of $\Sigma(X - \mu)$?
    a. 0
    b. $\sqrt{200}$
    c, 450
    d. cannot be determined from the information given

7. A population of $N = 10$ scores has $\mu = 50$ and SS = 200. For this population, what is the value of $\Sigma(X - \mu)^2$?
    a. 0
    b. 200
    c. $(450)^2$
    d. cannot be determined from the information given

8. A sample of $n = 10$ scores is selected from a population. The variability of the scores in the sample will tend to be _____ the variability of the scores in the population.
    a. less than
    b. greater than
    c. equal to

9. Sample variance provides an unbiased estimate of the population variance. The term *unbiased* means _____.
- a. for any sample, the sample variance will equal the population variance
- b. for large samples, the sample variance will equal the population variance
- c. if sample variance is computed for many samples, the average sample variance will equal the population variance
- d. None of the other choices is correct.

10. A sample of n = 4 scores has SS = 12. What is the standard deviation for the sample?
- a. 3
- b. the square root of 3
- c. 4
- d. the square root of 4

11. Without doing any serious calculations, which of the following samples has the largest variance?
- a. 1, 3, 4, 5, 6
- b. 1, 5, 8, 12, 22
- c. 30, 32, 34, 35, 36

12. A population of scores has $\mu = 20$ and $\sigma = 5$. If two points are added to every score in the population, then the new values for the mean and standard deviation would be _____.
- a. $\mu = 20$ and $\sigma = 5$
- b. $\mu = 22$ and $\sigma = 5$
- c. $\mu = 20$ and $\sigma = 7$
- d. $\mu = 22$ and $\sigma = 7$

13. A population of scores has $\mu = 20$ and $\sigma = 5$. If every score in the population is multiplied by 2, then the new values for the mean and standard deviation would be _____.
- a. $\mu = 20$ and $\sigma = 5$
- b. $\mu = 40$ and $\sigma = 5$
- c. $\mu = 20$ and $\sigma = 10$
- d. $\mu = 40$ and $\sigma = 10$

14. What is the variance for the following population of scores? Scores: 2, 2, 2, 2
- a. 0
- b. 2
- c. 4
- d. 16

15. If you have a score of X = 75 on an exam, which set of parameters would give you the highest position within the class?
    a. $\mu = 70$ and $\sigma = 5$
    b. $\mu = 70$ and $\sigma = 10$
    c. $\mu = 60$ and $\sigma = 5$
    d. $\mu = 60$ and $\sigma = 10$

Other Questions

1. Calculate the variance and standard deviation for the following sample of scores:
   7, 2, 4, 6, 4, 7, 3, 7

2. Compute the variance and standard deviation for the following population of scores:
   1, 9, 8, 5, 7

3. Calculate SS, variance, and standard deviation for the following sample of scores:
   15, 16, 9, 1, 9.

4. Describe what happens to the deviation scores and the standard deviation when a constant is added to every score in the distribution.

ANSWERS TO SELF TEST
True/False Answers

1. False. The range is 7 points.
2. True
3. True
4. True
5. False. Subtracting a constant will not change the standard deviation or the variance.
6. True
7. False. Divide SS by $n - 1$ for sample variance.
8. True
9. True
10. True

Multiple-Choice Answers

1. a The range is determined by the two most extreme scores in the distribution.
2. d All scores are used to compute the standard deviation.
3. c The deviations are 1, 2, and -3. The squared values sum to 14.
4. a SS is computed the same way for a sample or a population.
5. d The deviation is the distance. The sign indicates direction.
6. a $\Sigma(X - \mu)$ is the sum of the deviations and is always equal to zero.
7. b $\Sigma(X - \mu)^2$ is the sum of the squared deviations (SS).
8. a Sample variability is biased and tends to underestimate the population variability.
9. c An unbiased statistic will be equal to its corresponding parameter *on average*.
10. d Divide SS by $n - 1$ to obtain sample variance. Standard deviation is the square root of the variance.
11. b Variance measures how spread out the scores are.
12. b Adding a constant will cause the mean to change but has no effect on the standard deviation.
13. d Multiplying by a constant multiplies both the mean and the standard deviation.
14. a If all 4 scores are the same, then there is no variability (zero).
15. c Your score is three times the standard distance above the mean.

Other Answers

1. SS = 28, n = 8, df = 7, s^2 = 4, and s = 2

2. SS = 40, n = 5, σ^2 = 8, σ = 2.83

3. SS = 144, s^2 = 36, and s = 6

4. If a constant is added to each score, the mean also is increased by that constant. The deviation scores are not changed. If the deviation scores have not changed, then the squared deviations and SS will be unchanged. Thus, when a constant is added to every score in a distribution, the standard deviation is not changed.

CHAPTER 5

z-SCORES

CHAPTER SUMMARY

The goals of Chapter 5 are:
1. To introduce z-scores as a method for describing exact locations in a distribution.
2. To demonstrate how raw scores (X values) are transformed into z-scores, and how to reverse the transformation.
3. To demonstrate the concept of standardizing a distribution by transforming all of the scores into z-scores.
4. To demonstrate how z-scores can be used to create a standardized distribution with any predetermined values for the mean and standard deviation.

z-Scores and Location

By itself, a raw score or X value provides very little information about how that particular score compares with other values in the distribution. A score of X = 53, for example, may be a relatively low score, or an average score, or an extremely high score depending on the mean and standard deviation for the distribution from which the score was obtained. If the raw score is transformed into a z-score, however, the value of the z-score tells exactly where the score is located relative to all the other scores in the distribution. The process of changing an X value into a z-score involves creating a signed number, called a **z-score**, such that
  a. The sign of the z-score (+ or –) identifies whether the X value is located above the mean (positive) or below the mean (negative).
  b. The numerical value of the z-score corresponds to the number of standard deviations between X and the mean of the distribution.

Thus, a score that is located two standard deviations above the mean will have a z-score of +2.00. And, a z-score of +2.00 always indicates a location above the mean by two standard deviations.

Transforming back and forth between X and z

The basic z-score definition is usually sufficient to complete most z-score transformations. However, the definition can be written in mathematical notation to create a formula for computing the z-score for any value of X.

$$z = \frac{X - \mu}{\sigma}$$

Also, the terms in the formula can be regrouped to create an equation for computing the value of X corresponding to any specific z-score.

$$X = \mu + z\sigma$$

In addition to knowing the basic definition of a z-score and the formula for a z-score, it is useful to be able to visualize z-scores as locations in a distribution (see Figure 5.2 in the text). Remember, $z = 0$ is in the center (at the mean), and the extreme tails correspond to z-scores of approximately –2.00 on the left and +2.00 on the right. Although more extreme z-score values are possible, most of the distribution is contained between $z = -2.00$ and $z = +2.00$.

The fact that z-scores identify exact locations within a distribution, means that z-scores can be used as descriptive statistics and as inferential statistics. As descriptive statistics, z-scores describe exactly where each individual is located. As inferential statistics, z-scores determine whether a specific sample is representative of its population, or is extreme and unrepresentative. For example, a sample with a z-score near zero is a central, typical sample located near the population mean. On the other hand, a sample with a z-score value beyond 2.00 (or –2.00) would be considered an extreme or unusual sample, much different from the population mean.

z-Scores as a Standardized Distribution

When an entire distribution of X values is transformed into z-scores, the resulting distribution of z-scores will always have a mean of zero and a standard deviation of one. The transformation does not change the shape of the original distribution and it does not change the location of any individual score relative to others in the distribution.

The advantage of standardizing distributions is that two (or more) different distributions can be made the same. For example, one distribution has $\mu = 100$ and

$\sigma = 10$, and another distribution has $\mu = 40$ and $\sigma = 6$. When these distribution are transformed to z-scores, both will have $\mu = 0$ and $\sigma = 1$. Because z-score distributions all have the same mean and standard deviation, individual scores from different distributions can be directly compared. A z-score of $+1.00$ specifies the same location in all z-score distributions.

z-Scores and Samples

It is also possible to calculate z-scores for samples. The definition of a z-score is the same for either a sample or a population, and the formulas are also the same except that the sample mean and standard deviation are used in place of the population mean and standard deviation. Thus, for a score from a sample,

$$z = \frac{X - M}{s}$$

Using z-scores to standardize a sample also has the same effect as standardizing a population. Specifically, the mean of the z-scores will be zero and the standard deviation of the z-scores will be equal to 1.00 provided the standard deviation is computed using the sample formula (dividing $n - 1$ instead of n).

Other Standardized Distributions Based on z-Scores

Although transforming X values into z-scores creates a standardized distribution, many people find z-scores burdensome because they consist of many decimal values and negative numbers. Therefore, it is often more convenient to standardize a distribution into numerical values that are simpler than z-scores. To create a simpler standardized distribution, you first select the mean and standard deviation that you would like for the new distribution. Then, z-scores are used to identify each individual's position in the original distribution and to compute the individual's position in the new distribution. Suppose, for example, that you want to standardize a distribution so that the new mean is $\mu = 50$ and the new standard deviation is $\sigma = 10$. An individual with $z = -1.00$ in the original distribution would be assigned a score of $X = 40$ (below μ by one standard deviation) in the standardized distribution. Repeating this process for each individual score allows you to transform an entire distribution into a new, standardized distribution.

LEARNING OBJECTIVES

1. You should be able to describe and understand the purpose for z-scores.

2. You should be able to transform X values into z-scores or transform z-scores into X values.

3. You should be able to describe the effects of standardizing a distribution by transforming the entire set of raw scores into z-scores.

4. Using z-scores, you should be able to transform any set of scores into a distribution with a predetermined mean and standard deviation.

NEW TERMS AND CONCEPTS

The following terms were introduced in this chapter. You should be able to define or describe each term and, where appropriate, describe how each term is related to other terms in the list.

raw score	An original, untransformed observation or measurement.
z-score	A standardized score with a sign that indicates direction from the mean (+ above μ and $-$ below μ), and a numerical value equal to the distance from the mean measured in standard deviations.
z-score transformation	A transformation that changes raw scores (X values) into z-scores.
standard score	A score that has been transformed into a standard form.
standardized distribution	An entire distribution that has been transformed to create predetermined values for μ and σ.

NEW FORMULAS

For a population:

$$z = \frac{X - \mu}{\sigma}$$

$$X = \mu + z\sigma$$

For a sample:

$$z = \frac{X - M}{s}$$

$$X = M + zs$$

STEP BY STEP

Changing X to z: The process of changing an X value to a z-score involves finding the precise location of X within its distribution. We will begin with a distribution with $\mu = 60$ and $\sigma = 12$. The goal is to find the z-score for X = 75.

Step 1: First determine whether X is above or below the mean. This will determine the sign of the z-score. For our example, X is above μ so the z-score will be positive.

Step 2: Next, find the distance between X and μ. For our example,
$$X - \mu = 75 - 60 = 15 \text{ points}$$
Note: Steps 1 and 2 simply determine a deviation score (sign and magnitude). If you are using the z-score formula, these two steps correspond to the numerator of the equation.

Step 3: Convert the distance from Step 2 into standard deviation units. In the z-score equation, this step corresponds to dividing by σ. For this example,
$$15/12 = 1.25$$

If you are using the z-score definition (rather than the formula), you simply compare the magnitude of the distance (Step 2) with the magnitude of the standard deviation. For this example, our distance of 15 points is equal to one standard deviation plus 3 more points. The extra 3 points are equal to one-quarter of a standard deviation, so the total distance is one and one-quarter standard deviations.

Step 4: Combine the sign from Step 1 with the number of standard deviations you obtained in Step 3. For this example,
$$z = +1.25$$

Changing z to X: The process of converting a z-score into an X value corresponds to finding the score that is located at a specified position in a distribution. Again, suppose we have a population with $\mu = 60$ and $\sigma = 12$. What is the X value corresponding to $z = -0.50$?

Step 1: The sign of the z-score tells whether X is above or below the mean. For this example, the X value we want is below μ.

Step 2: The magnitude of the z-score tells how many standard deviations there are between X and μ. For this example, the distance is one-half a standard deviation which is $(1/2)(12) = 6$ points.

Step 3: Starting with the value of the mean, use the direction (Step 1) and the distance (Step 2) to determine the X value. For this example, we want to find the score that is 6 points below $\mu = 60$. Therefore,
$$X = 60 - 6 = 54$$

HINTS AND CAUTIONS

1. Rather than memorizing formulas for z-scores, we suggest that you rely on the definition of a z-score. Remember a z-score identifies a location by specifying the direction from the mean (+ or –) and the distance from the mean in terms of standard deviations.

2. When transforming scores from X to z (or from z to X) it is wise to check your answer by reversing the transformation. For example, given a population with $\mu = 54$ and $\sigma = 4$ a score of $X = 46$ corresponds to a z-score of

$$z = \frac{X - \mu}{\sigma} = \frac{46 - 54}{4} = \frac{-8}{4} = -2.00$$

To check this answer, convert the z-score back into an X value. In this case, $z = -2.00$ specifies a location below the mean by 2 standard deviations. This distance is
$$z\sigma = -2.00(4) = -8 \text{ points}$$

With a mean of $\mu = 54$, the score must be

$$X = 54 - 8 = 46.$$

SELF TEST

True/False Questions

1. A positive z-score always corresponds to a score greater than the mean.

2. For any distribution, a z-score of z = –0.50 corresponds to a location below the mean.

T

3. In a distribution with $\mu = 50$ and $\sigma = 10$, a score of X = 55 corresponds to a z-score of z = +0.50.

$$\frac{55 - 50}{10} \quad \frac{5}{10} \quad .5 \quad + $$

4. For a sample with M = 40 and s = 12, a z-score of z = –0.50 corresponds to a score of X = 46.

$$-.50 = \frac{46 - 40}{12} \quad \frac{6}{12} \quad F$$

5. One advantage of transforming X values into z-scores is that the transformation always creates a normal distribution.

F

6. In a sample with s = 8, a score of X = 64 corresponds to z = –0.50. The mean for this sample is M = 60.

7. In a distribution with $\mu = 80$, a score of X = 70 corresponds to z = –0.50. The standard deviation for this population is $\sigma = 5$.

8. A population with $\mu = 100$ and $\sigma = 20$ is transformed into z-scores. The resulting distribution of z-scores will have a mean of zero.

9. A z-score of –2.00 always indicates a more extreme location (farther from the mean) than a z-score of –1.00.

10. A population with $\mu = 37$ and $\sigma = 6$ is standardized to create a new distribution with $\mu = 100$ and $\sigma = 20$. In this transformation, a score of X = 43 from the original distribution will be transformed into a score of X = 120.

Multiple-Choice Questions

1. For a population with $\mu = 100$ and $\sigma = 20$, what is the z-score corresponding to X = 105?
    a. +0.25
    b. +0.50
    c. +4.00
    d. +5.00

2. For a sample with M = 100 and s = 20, what is the X value corresponding to
z = –0.25?

      a. 99.75

      b. 97.5

      c. 95

      d. 92.5

3. A z-score of z = –2.00 indicates a position

      a. below the mean by 2 points

      b. below the mean by 2 times the standard deviation

      c. above the mean by 2 points

      d. above the mean by 2 times the standard deviation

4. A population has a standard deviation of $\sigma = 6$. In this distribution, a score that is 12
points above the mean would correspond to a z-score of _____.

      a. z = 1

      b. z = 2

      c. z = 6

      d. z = 12

$$\sigma = 12 \qquad 2 = x\ \frac{-12}{6}$$

$$12 + 12 \atop 24 = x$$

5.   For a population with a mean of $\mu = 70$, a score that is located 10 points below the
mean would have a z-score of _____.

      a. +1

      b. –1

      c. –10

      d. cannot answer without knowing the standard deviation

6.   A population of scores has $\sigma = 10$. In this population, a score of X = 60 corresponds
to z = –1.50. What is the population mean?

      a. –30

      b. 45

      c. 75

      d. 90

7. A population of scores has $\mu = 50$. In this population, an X value of 58 corresponds to
    z = 2.00.   What is the population standard deviation?

      a. 2

      b. 4

      c. 8

      d. 16

8. Under what circumstances would a score that is 15 points above the mean be considered to be near the center of the distribution?
   a. when the population mean is much larger than 15
   b. when the population standard deviation is much larger than 15
   c. when the population mean is much smaller than 15
   d. when the population standard deviation is much smaller than 15

9. A z-score of $z = -0.25$ indicates a location that is _____.
   a. at the center of the distribution
   b. slightly below the mean
   c. far below the mean in the extreme left-hand tail of the distribution
   d. the location depends on the mean and standard deviation for the distribution

10. A population with $\mu = 85$ and $\sigma = 12$ is transformed into z-scores. After the transformation, the population of z-scores will have a mean of _____.
   a. $\mu = 85$
   b. $\mu = 1.00$
   c. $\mu = 0$
   d. cannot be determined from the information given

11. A population has $\mu = 50$. What value of σ would make $X = 55$ an extreme score in this population?
   a. $\sigma = 1$
   b. $\sigma = 5$
   c. $\sigma = 10$
   d. cannot determine with the information given

12. You have a score of $X = 65$ on an exam. Which set of parameters would give you the best grade on the exam?
   a. $\mu = 60$ and $\sigma = 10$
   b. $\mu = 60$ and $\sigma = 5$
   c. $\mu = 70$ and $\sigma = 10$
   d. $\mu = 70$ and $\sigma = 5$

13. Which of the following is an advantage of transforming X values into z-scores?
   a. All negative numbers are eliminated.
   b. The distribution is transformed to a normal shape.
   c. All scores are moved closer to the mean.
   d. None of the other options is an advantage.

14. A distribution with $\mu = 35$ and $\sigma = 8$ is being standardized so that the new mean and standard deviation will be $\mu = 50$ and $\sigma = 10$. When the distribution is standardized, what value will be obtained for a score of $X = 39$ from the original distribution?
   a. $X = 54$
   b. $X = 55$
   c. $X = 1.10$
   d. impossible to determine without more information

15. A distribution with $\mu = 35$ and $\sigma = 8$ is being standardized so that the new mean and standard deviation will be $\mu = 50$ and $\sigma = 10$. In the new, standardized distribution your score is $X = 60$. What was your score in the original distribution?
   a. $X = 45$
   b. $X = 43$
   c. $X = 1.00$
   d. impossible to determine without more information

Other Questions

1. For a population with $\mu = 90$ and $\sigma = 25$, find the z-score corresponding to each of the following X values.
   a. $X = 95$
   b. $X = 110$
   c. $X = 65$
   d. $X = 80$

2. For a sample with $M = 60$ and $s = 6$, find the X value corresponding to each of the following z-scores.
   a. $z = +1.50$
   b. $z = -0.50$
   c. $z = +2.00$
   d. $z = -1/3$

3. On an exam with $\mu = 70$ and $\sigma = 10$, you have a score of $X = 85$.
   a. What is your z-score on this exam?
   b. If the instructor added 5 points to every score, what would happen to your z-score?
   c. If the instructor multiplied every score by 2, what would happen to your z-score?

4. A set of exam scores has $\mu = 48$ and $\sigma = 8$. The instructor would like to transform the scores into a standardized distribution with $\mu = 100$ and $\sigma = 20$. Find the transformed value for each of the following scores from the original population.
   a. $X = 48$
   b. $X = 50$
   c. $X = 44$
   d. $X = 32$

ANSWERS TO SELF TEST

True/False Answers

1. True
2. True
3. True
4. False. The score is below the mean: $X = 34$
5. False. Changing X to z does not change the shape of the distribution.
6. False. The score is below the mean: $M = 68$.
7. False. One half of the standard deviation is 10: $\sigma = 20$.
8. True
9. True
10. True

Multiple-Choice Answers

1. a $X = 105$ is above the mean (+) by exactly 0.25 standard deviations.
2. c 0.25 standard deviations is exactly 5 points below the mean.
3. b The z-score identifies the direction and distance from the mean in terms of the number of standard deviations.
4. b 12 points is exactly 2 standard deviations.
5. d You cannot compute a z-score without knowing the standard deviation.
6. c 1.5 standard deviations is 15 points below the mean, so $\mu = 75$.
7. b If 8 points is two standard deviations, then $\sigma = 4$.
8. b 15 points is a small distance when the standard deviation is more than 15.
9. b The location is below the mean by 0.25 standard deviations.
10. c Transforming X value to z-scores always produces a mean of zero.
11. a Five points is an extreme distance with $\sigma = 1$.
12. b $\mu = 60$ and $\sigma = 5$ produce the largest z-score.

13. d None of these characteristics is associated with z-scores.
14. b X = 39 corresponds to z = 0.50. In the new distribution this location corresponds to X = 55.
15. b X = 60 corresponds to z = 1.00. In the old distribution this location corresponds to X = 43.

Other Answers

1. a. z = +0.20
   b. z = +0.80
   c. z = −1.00
   d. z = −0.40

2. a. X = 69   c. X = 72
   b. X = 57   d. X = 58

3. a. Your z-score is z = 1.50.
   b. Adding 5 points to every score would increase your score and the mean by 5 points. However, your z-score (your position within the distribution) would not change.
   c. Multiplying every score by 2 will multiply the mean, the standard deviation, and your score. However, your z-score (your position within the distribution) will not change.

4 a. X = 48 corresponds to z = 0. In the new distribution this location corresponds to X = 100.
   b. X = 50 corresponds to z = +0.25 which corresponds to X = 105 in the new distribution.
   c. X = 44 corresponds to z = −0.50. X = 90 in the new distribution.
   d. X = 32 corresponds to z = −2.00. X = 60 in the new distribution.

CHAPTER 6

PROBABILITY

CHAPTER SUMMARY

The goals of Chapter 6 are:
1. To introduce the concept of probability.
2. To demonstrate how the unit normal table can be used to find the proportions of a normal distribution corresponding to any specific z-score location.
3. To demonstrate how the combination of z-scores and the unit normal table can be used to find probabilities any score (X value) from a normal distribution, and how the table can be used to find the score corresponding to any specific proportion.
4. To demonstrate how probability will be used as part of the inferential statistics in future chapters.

Probability

In this chapter we introduce the concept of probability as a method for measuring and quantifying the likelihood of obtaining a specific sample from a specific population. We define probability as a fraction or a proportion. In particular, the probability of any specific outcome is determined by a ratio comparing the frequency of occurrence for that outcome relative to the total number of possible outcomes.

Whenever the scores in a population are variable it is impossible to predict with perfect accuracy exactly which score or scores will be obtained when you take a sample from the population. In this situation researchers rely on probability to determine the relative likelihood for specific samples. Thus, although a researcher may not be able to predict exactly which value(s) will be obtained for a sample, it is possible to determine exactly which outcomes have high probability and which have low probability.

Probability is determined by a fraction or proportion. When a population of scores is represented by a frequency distribution, probabilities can be defined by proportions of the distribution. In graphs, probability can be defined as a proportion of area under the curve.

Probability and the Normal Distribution

If a vertical line is drawn through a normal distribution, several things occur.

1. The exact location of the line can be specified by a z-score.
2. The line divides the distribution into two sections. The larger section is called the **body** and the smaller section is called the **tail**.

The **unit normal table** lists several different proportions corresponding to each z-score location. Column A of the table lists z-score values. For each z-score location, columns B and C list the proportions in the body and tail, respectively. Finally, column D lists the proportion between the mean and the z-score location. Because probability is equivalent to proportion, the table values can also be used to determine probabilities.

To find the probability corresponding to a particular score (X value), you first transform the score into a z-score, then look up the z-score in the table and read across the row to find the appropriate proportion/probability. To find the score (X value) corresponding to a particular proportion, you first look up the proportion in the table, read across the row to find the corresponding z-score, and then transform the z-score into an X value.

Percentiles and Percentile Ranks

In Box 6.1 we noted that the **percentile rank** for a specific X value is the percentage of individuals with scores at or below that value. When a score is referred to by its rank, the score is called a **percentile**. The percentile rank for a score in a normal distribution is simply the proportion to the left of the score.

Probability and Inferential Statistics

Probability is important because it establishes a link between samples and populations. For any known population it is possible to determine the probability of obtaining any specific sample. In later chapters we will use this link as the foundation for inferential statistics. The general goal of inferential statistics is to use the information from a sample to reach a general conclusion (inference) about an unknown population. Typically a researcher begins with a sample. If the sample has a high probability of being obtained from a specific population, then the researcher can conclude that the sample is likely to have come from that population. On the other hand, if the sample has a very low probability of being obtained from a specific population, then it is reasonable for the researcher to conclude that the specific population is probably not the source for the sample.

LEARNING OBJECTIVES

1. Know how to determine the probability of an event.

2. Be able to use the unit normal table to determine the probabilities for events that are normally distributed.

3. Be able to combine z-score calculations (Chapter 5) and the unit normal table to find probabilities for scores from a normal distribution, or to find the scores associated with specific proportions.

NEW TERMS AND CONCEPTS

The following terms were introduced in this chapter. You should be able to define or describe each term and, where appropriate, describe how each term is related to other terms in the list.

probability	Probability is defined as a proportion, a specific part out of the whole set of possibilities.
proportion	A part of the whole usually expressed as a fraction.
random sample	A sample obtained using a process that gives every individual an equal chance of being selected and keeps the probability of being selected constant over a series of selections.
sampling with replacement	A sampling technique that returns the current selection to the population before the next selection is made. A required part of random sampling.
normal distribution	A symmetrical, bell-shaped distribution with proportions corresponding to those listed in the unit normal table.
unit normal table	A table listing proportions corresponding to each z-score location in a normal distribution.

NEW FORMULAS

$$p(A) = \frac{\text{Number of ways event A can occur}}{\text{Total number of possible outcomes}}$$

STEP BY STEP

Finding the probability associated with a specified score. The general process involves converting the score (X) into a z-score, then using the unit normal table to find the probability associated with the z-score. To demonstrate this process, we will find the probability of randomly selecting a score greater than 95 from a normal distribution with $\mu = 100$ and $\sigma = 10$.

Step 1: Sketch the distribution and identify the mean and standard deviation. Then, find the approximate location of the specified score and draw a vertical line through the distribution. For this example, X = 95 is located below the mean by roughly one-half of the standard deviation.

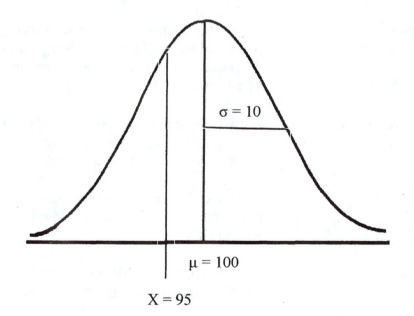

Step 2:   Read the problem again to determine whether you want the proportion greater than the score (right of your line) or less than the score (left of the line). Then shade in the appropriate portion of the distribution. For this example we want the proportion consisting of scores greater than 95, so shade in the portion to the right of X = 95.

Step 3:   Look at your sketch and make an estimate of the proportion that has been shaded. Remember, the mean divides the distribution in half with 50% on each side. For this example, we have shaded more than 50% of the distribution. The shaded area appears to be about 60% or 70% of the distribution.

Step 4:   Transform the X value into a z-score. For this example, X = 95 corresponds to z = –0.50.

Step 5:   Look up the z-score value in the unit normal table. (Ignore the + or – sign.) Find the proportions in the table that correspond to your z-score. Usually, the proportions in the tail (column C) and in the body (column B) will be sufficient to find the answer. Write these two proportions in the appropriate places on your figure.

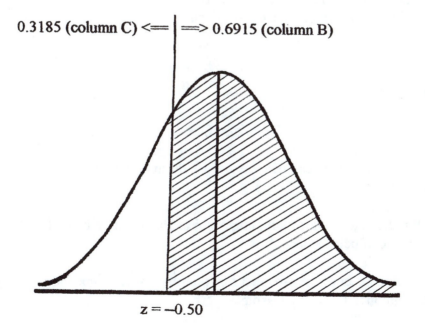

0.3185 (column C) <== | ==> 0.6915 (column B)

z = –0.50

Step 6:   You must use the proportions from the table to find the value that corresponds to the shaded area of your figure. For this example, the column B proportion, 0.6915, corresponds to the shaded area.

Step 7:   Compare your final answer with the estimate you made in Step 4. If your answer does not agree with your preliminary estimate, re-work the problem.

HINTS AND CAUTIONS

1. In using probability, you should be comfortable in converting fractions into decimals or percentages. These values all represent ways of expressing portions of the whole. If you have difficulty with fractions or decimals, review the section on proportions in the math review appendix of your textbook.

2. It usually helps to restate a probability problem as a question about proportion. For example, the problem, "What is the probability of selecting an ace from a deck of cards?" becomes, "What proportion of the deck is composed of aces?"

3. When using the unit normal table to answer probability questions, you should always start by sketching a normal distribution and shading in the area of the distribution for which you need a proportion.

SELF TEST

True/False Questions

1. The value for a probability can never exceed 1.00, unless you have made a computational error.

2. As defined in the text, random sampling requires that each individual in the population has an equal chance of being selected.

3. Sampling with replacement means that it is possible for the same individual to be selected more than once for a single sample.

4. The definition of a random sample in the text requires sampling with replacement.

5. If there are 10 seniors and 40 juniors in a class, then the probability of randomly selecting a senior is p(senior) = 1/4. *F*

2/30

6. A jar contains 10 red marbles and 20 blue marbles. If you take a *random sample* of two marbles from this jar, then the probability that the second marble is blue does *not* depend on the color of the first marble. *T*

7. For any normal distribution, the proportion in the tail beyond z = –2.00 is p = –0.0228.

8. For any normal distribution, exactly 2.5% of the scores are located in the tail beyond z = 1.96.

9. For a normal distribution, a z-score of –1.28 separates the top 10.03% from the rest of the distribution.

10. For a normal distribution, the proportion in the tail beyond z = +1.00 is exactly the same as the proportion in the tail beyond z = –1.00.

Multiple-Choice Questions

1. A colony of laboratory rats contains 7 albino rats and 23 hooded rats. What is the probability of randomly selecting an albino rat from this colony?
    a. 7/23
    b. 7/30
    c. 23/30
    d. 23/7

7/30

2. A jar contains 40 red marbles and 10 black marbles. If you take a *random sample* of n = 3 marbles from this jar, and the first two marbles are both red, what is the probability that the third marble will be black?
    a. 10/50
    b. 9/49
    c. 10/49
    d. either 9/49 or 10/49

40R < 1M
      2M
50B

N=3

3. The proportion of a normal distribution that corresponds to values less than z = 1.00 is p = 0.8413. Base on this information, what is the proportion that corresponds to values greater than z = –1.00?
    a. 0.8413
    b. –0.8413
    c. 0.1587
    d. –0.1587

4. For a normal distribution, what z-score value separates the highest 10% of the distribution from the lowest 90%?
    a. z = 0.90
    b. z = –0.90
    c. z = 1.28
    d. z = –1.28

5. What percentage of a normal distribution is located in the tail beyond z = 2.00?
    a. 1.14%
    b. 2%
    c. 2.28%
    d. 97.72%

6. If the tail of a normal distribution contains exactly 2.5% of the scores, then what is the z-score value that separates the tail from the body of the distribution?
    a. z = 1.96
    b. z = –1.96
    c. either z = 1.96 or z = –1.96
    d. none of the above is correct

7. A normal distribution has a mean of μ = 60 with σ = 8. What is the probability of selecting an individual with a score greater than 54?
    a. 0.2266
    b. 0.7734
    c. 0.7266
    d. 0.2734

$$\frac{54-60}{8} \quad \frac{-6}{8} = -.75$$

8. For a normal distribution with μ = 90 and σ = 5, what is p(X < 84)?
    a. 11.51%
    b. 54%
    c. 38.49%
    d. 88.49%

$$\frac{84-90}{5} \quad -1.2$$

9. A normal distribution has $\mu = 100$ and $\sigma = 20$. What score separates the top 40% from the rest of the distribution?

    a. X = 110
    b. X = 105
    c. X = 90
    d. X = 95

$$\frac{110 - 100}{20}$$

$$\frac{10}{20} \quad \cdot 5$$

10. For any normal distribution, what z-score separates the top 60% from the rest of the distribution?

    a. z = 1.28
    b. z = -1.28
    c. z = 0.25
    d. z = -0.25

11. Scores on the SAT form a normal distribution with a mean of $\mu = 500$ and $\sigma = 100$. In this distribution, what percentage of the individuals have scores less than X = 450?

    a. 19.15%
    b. 30.85%
    c. 69.15%
    d. 80.85%

$$\frac{450 - 500}{100}$$

$$\frac{-50}{100} \quad -.5$$

$$\cdot 3085$$

12. For a normal distribution with $\mu = 500$ and $\sigma = 100$, what score separates the top 20% of the distribution from the rest?

    a. 372
    b. 628
    c. 416
    d. 584

$$\frac{628 - 500}{100}$$

$$584 - 500 \qquad 1.28$$

$$\frac{416 - 500}{} \quad -.84$$

13. For any normal distribution, the middle 50% is bounded by z-score values of

    a. z = ±0.25
    b. z = ±0.50
    c. z = ±0.67
    d. z = ±1.00

14. Scores on the SAT form a normal distribution with $\mu = 500$ and $\sigma = 100$. What is the minimum SAT score needed to be in the top 10% of the distribution?

    a. X = 525
    b. X = 590
    c. X = 628
    d. X = 733

$$2.33$$

15. For a normal distribution with $\mu = 100$ and $\sigma = 10$, what scores (X values) separate the middle 95% from the rest?
   a. X = 83.5 and X = 116.5
   b. X = 80.4 and X = 119.6
   c. X = 87.2 and X = 112.8
   d. X = 95 and X = 105

Other Questions

1. Assume a normal distribution for each question.
   a. What proportion of the distribution consists of z-scores greater than 0.25?
   b. What is the probability of obtaining a z-score less than 0.50?
   c. What is the probability of obtaining a z-score greater than -1.50?
   d. What is the probability of obtaining a z-score between $+1.00$ and -1.00?

2. Find the z-score that separates a normal distribution into the following two portions:
   a. separate the lowest 80% from the highest 20%
   b. separate the lowest 90% from the highest 10%
   c. separate the lowest 15% from the highest 85%
   d. separate the lowest 40% from the highest 60%

3. Find the following probabilities for a normal distribution with $\mu = 80$ and $\sigma = 12$.
   a. $p(X > 86)$
   b. $p(X > 77)$
   c. $p(X < 95)$
   d. $p(X < 68)$

4. For a normal distribution with $\mu = 80$ and $\sigma = 12$, find the X value associated with each of the following proportions:
   a. What X value separates the distribution into the top 40% versus the bottom 60%?
   b. What is the minimum X value needed to be in the top 25% of the distribution?
   c. What X value separates the top 60% from the bottom 40% of the distribution?

ANSWERS TO SELF TEST

True/False Answers

1. True
2. True
3. True
4. True
5. False. The probability would be 10/50 because there are 50 students.
6. True
7. False. Proportions are always positive: p = 0.0228.
8. True
9. False. 89.97% have scores greater than z = –1.28.
10. True

Multiple-Choice Answers

1. b   There are 7 albinos out of a total of 30 rats.
2. a   Remember, a *random sample* includes sampling with replacement.
3. a   The distribution is symmetrical.
4. c   With 0.1000 in the right-hand tail, the z-score is z = 1.28.
5. c   The proportion in the tail is 0.0228.
6. c   The 2.5% could be in either tail.
7. b   X = 54 corresponds to z = –0.75 which has 0.7734 in the body.
8. a   X = 84 corresponds to z = –1.20 which has 0.1151 in the tail.
9. b   With 0.4000 in the right-hand tail, z = +0.25 and X = 105.
10. d   The boundary for the top 60% is z = –0.25.
11. b   X = 450 corresponds to z = –0.50 which has 0.3085 in the tail.
12. d   The top 20% corresponds to z = 0.84 which corresponds to X = 584.
13. c   The closest value is z = ±0.67 which has a proportion of .2514 between the mean and the z-score on both sides.
14. c   The top 10% corresponds to z = 1.28 which corresponds to X = 628.
15. b   The middle 95% corresponds to z = ±1.96.

Other Answers

1 a. p(z > 0.25) = 0.4013
   b. p(z < 0.50) = 0.6915
   c. p(z > –1.50) = 0.9332
   d. p(–1.00 < z > 1.00) = 0.6826

2. a. $z = 0.84$ c. $z = -1.04$
   b. $z = 1.28$ d. $z = -0.25$

3. a. $z = 0.50$ and $p = 0.3085$
   b. $z = -0.25$ and $p = 0.5987$
   c. $z = 1.25$ and $p = 0.8944$
   d. $z = -1.00$ and $p = 0.1587$

4. a. $z = 0.25$ and $X = 83$
   b. $z = 0.67$ and $X = 88.04$
   c. $z = -0.25$ and $X = 77$

CHAPTER 7

THE DISTRIBUTION OF SAMPLE MEANS

CHAPTER SUMMARY

The goals for Chapter 7 are:
1. To introduce the distribution of sample means and identify its parameters.
2. To demonstrate how z-scores can be used to identify the location of a specific sample mean within the distribution of sample means.
3. To demonstrate how the unit normal table can be used to find probabilities for sample means.
4. To introduce the concept of standard error as a critical component of inferential statistics.

The Distribution of Sample Means

In the previous two chapters we presented the statistical procedures for computing z-scores and finding probabilities associated with individual scores, X-values. In order to find z-scores or probabilities, the first requirement is that you must know about *all the possible X values*, that is, the entire distribution. A z-score tells where an individual X is located relative to all the other X values in the distribution. To find a probability, we simply identified a proportion of all the possible X values.

In Chapter 7 we extend the concepts of z-scores and probability to samples of more than one score. Specifically, we will compute z-scores and find probabilities for sample means. To accomplish this task, the first requirement is that you must know about *all the possible sample means*, that is, the entire distribution of Ms. Once this distribution is identified, then
1. A z-score can be computed for each sample mean. The z-score tells where the specific sample mean is located relative to all the other sample means.
2. The probability associated with a specific sample mean can be defined as a proportion of all the possible sample means.

The **distribution of sample means** is defined as the set of means from all the possible random samples of a specific size (n) selected from a specific population. This distribution has well-defined (and predictable) characteristics that are specified in the Central Limit Theorem:

1. The mean of the distribution of sample means is called the **Expected Value of M** and is always equal to the population mean μ.

2. The standard deviation of the distribution of sample means is called the **Standard Error of M** and is computed by

$$\sigma_M = \frac{\sigma}{\sqrt{n}} \qquad \text{or} \qquad \sigma_M = \frac{\sigma^2}{n}$$

3. The shape of the distribution of sample means tends to be normal. It is guaranteed to be normal if either a) the population from which the samples are obtained is normal, or b) the sample size is n = 30 or more.

The concept of the distribution of sample means and its characteristics should be intuitively reasonable. First, you should realize that sample means are variable. If two (or more) samples are selected from the same population, the two samples probably will have different means. Second, although the samples will have different means, you should expect the sample means to be close to the population mean. That is, the sample means should "pile up" around μ. Thus, the distribution of sample means tends to form a normal shape with an expected value of μ. Finally, you should realize that an individual sample mean probably will not be identical to its population mean; that is, there will be some "error" between M and μ. Some sample means will be relatively close to μ and others will be relatively far away. The standard error provides a measure of the standard distance between M and μ.

z-Scores and Location within the Distribution of Sample Means

Within the distribution of sample means, the location of each sample mean can be specified by a z-score,

$$z = \frac{M - \mu}{\sigma_M}$$

As always, a positive z-score indicates a sample mean that is greater than μ and a negative z-score corresponds to a sample mean that is smaller than μ. The numerical value of the z-score indicates the distance between M and μ measured in terms of the standard error.

Probability and Sample Means

Because the distribution of sample means tends to be normal, the z-score value obtained for a sample mean can be used with the unit normal table to obtain probabilities. The procedures for computing z-scores and finding probabilities for sample means are essentially the same as we used for individual scores (in Chapters 5 and 6). However, when you are using sample means, you must remember to consider the sample size (n) and compute the standard error (σ_M) before you start any other computations. Also, you must be sure that the distribution of sample means satisfies at least one of the criteria for normal shape before you can use the unit normal table.

The Standard Error of M

Standard error is perhaps the single most important concept in inferential statistics. The standard error of M is defined as the standard deviation of the distribution of sample means and measures the standard distance between a sample mean and the population mean. Thus, the Standard Error of M provides a measure of how accurately, on average, a sample mean represents its corresponding population mean.

The magnitude of the standard error is determined by two factors: σ and n. The population standard deviation, σ, measures the standard distance between a single score (X) and the population mean. Thus, the standard deviation provides a measure of the "error" that is expected for the smallest possible sample, when n = 1. As the sample size is increased, it is reasonable to expect that the error should decrease. In simple terms, the larger the sample, the more accurately it should represent its population. The formula for standard error reflects the intuitive relationship between standard deviation, sample size, and "error."

$$\sigma_M = \frac{\sigma}{\sqrt{n}}$$

As the sample size increases, the error decreases. As the sample size decreases, the error increases. At the extreme, when n = 1, the error is equal to the standard deviation.

LEARNING OBJECTIVES

1. For any specific sampling situation, you should be able to define and describe the distribution of sample means by identifying its shape, the expected value of M, and the standard error of M.

2. You should be able to define and calculate the standard error of M.

3. You should be able to compute a z-score that specifies the location of a particular sample mean within the distribution of sample means.

4. Using the distribution of sample means, you should be able to compute the probability of obtaining specific values for a sample mean obtained from a given population.

5. You should be able to incorporate a visual presentation of standard error into a graph presenting means for a set of different samples. In addition, you should be able to use the visual presentation of standard error to help determine whether the obtained difference between two sample means reflects a "real" difference in the populations, or whether the sample mean difference is simply due to chance.

NEW TERMS AND CONCEPTS

The following terms were introduced in this chapter. You should be able to define or describe each term and, where appropriate, describe how each term is related to other terms in the list.

distribution of sample means	The set of sample means from all the possible random samples for a specific sample size (n) from a specific population.
sampling distribution	A distribution of statistics (as opposed to a distribution of scores). The distribution of sample means is an example of a sampling distribution.
expected value of M	The mean of the distribution of sample means. The average of the M values.
standard error of M	The standard deviation of the distribution of sample means. The standard distance between a sample mean and the population mean.
the central limit theorem	A mathematical theorem that specifies the characteristics of the distribution of sample means.

NEW FORMULAS

$$\sigma_M = \frac{\sigma}{\sqrt{n}} \qquad \text{or} \qquad \sigma_M = \sqrt{\frac{\sigma^2}{n}}$$

$$z = \frac{M - \mu}{\sigma_M}$$

STEP BY STEP

Computing Probabilities for Sample Means: You should recall that we have defined probability as being equivalent to proportion. Thus, the probability associated with a specific sample mean can be defined as a specific proportion of the distribution of sample means. Because the distribution of sample means tends to be normal, you can use z-scores and the unit normal table to determine proportions or probabilities. The following example demonstrates the details of this process.

For a normal population with $\mu = 60$ and $\sigma = 12$, what is the probability of selecting a random sample of $n = 36$ scores with a sample mean greater than 64? In symbols, $p(M > 64) = ?$

Step 1: Rephrase the probability question as a proportion question. For this example, "Out of all the possible sample means for $n = 36$, what proportion have values greater than 64?"

Step 2: We are looking for a specific proportion of "all the possible sample means." The set of "all possible sample means" is the distribution of sample means. Therefore, the next step is to sketch the distribution. Show the expected value and standard error in your sketch. Caution: Be sure to use the standard error, not the standard deviation.

For this example, the distribution of sample means will have an expected value of $\mu = 60$, a standard error of $\sigma_M = 12/\sqrt{36} = 2$, and it will be a normal distribution because the original population is normal (also because $n > 30$).

Caution: If the distribution of sample means is not normal, you cannot use the unit normal table to find probabilities.

Step 3: Find the approximate location of the specified sample mean and draw a vertical line through the distribution. For this example, M = 64 is located above the mean by roughly two times the standard deviation.

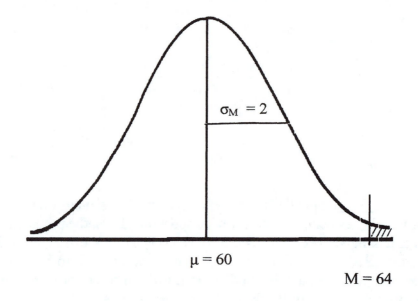

$$\sigma_M = 2$$

$$\mu = 60$$

$$M = 64$$

Step 4: Determine whether the problem asked for the proportion greater than or less than the specific M. Then shade in the appropriate area in your sketch. For this example, we want the area greater than M = 64 so shade in the area on the right-hand side of the line.

Step 5: Look at your sketch and make a preliminary estimate of the proportion that is shaded. For this example, we have shaded a very small part of the whole distribution, probably 5% or less.

Step 6: Compute the z-score for the specified sample mean. Be sure to use the z-score formula for sample means. For this example, M = 64 corresponds to z = +2.00.

$$z = \frac{M - \mu}{\sigma_M} = \frac{64 - 60}{2} = \frac{4}{2} = 2.00$$

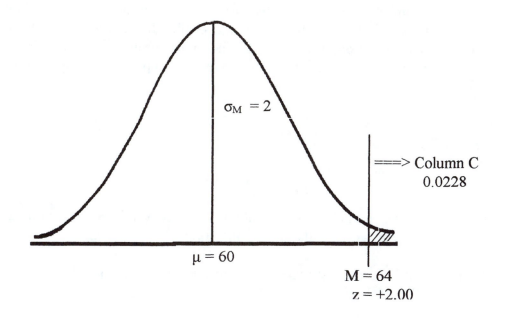

$\sigma_M = 2$

===> Column C
0.0228

$\mu = 60$

M = 64
z = +2.00

Step 7:   Look up the z-score in the unit normal table and find the two proportions in columns B and C. For this example, the value in column C (the tail of the distribution) corresponds exactly to the proportion we want.
  p(M > 64) = p(z > +2.00) = .0228

Step 8:   Compare your final answer with the preliminary estimate from Step 5. Be sure that your answer is in agreement with the common-sense estimate you made earlier.

HINTS AND CAUTIONS

1.   Whenever you encounter a question about a sample mean you must remember to use the distribution of sample means and not the original population distribution. The population distribution contains scores (not sample means) and therefore should be used only when you have a question about an individual score (n = 1).

2. The key to working with the distribution of sample means is the standard error of M:

$$\sigma_M = \frac{\sigma}{\sqrt{n}}$$

Remember, larger samples tend to be more accurate (less error) than smaller samples: The larger the sample, the smaller the difference between the sample mean and the population mean. The sample size, n, is a crucial factor in determining the standard error between a sample and its population.

SELF TEST

True/False Questions

1. Two samples probably will have different means even if they are both the same size and they are both selected from the same population.

2. It is possible for the distribution of sample means to be normal even if it is based on samples with less than $n = 30$.

3. The mean of the distribution of sample means is called the *standard error of M*.

4. If a sample consists of at least $n = 30$ scores, then the sample mean will be equal to the population mean.

5. A population has $\mu = 80$ and $\sigma = 20$. The distribution of sample means based on samples of $n = 4$ selected from this population will have a standard error of 5.

6. A population has $\mu = 80$ and $\sigma = 20$. The distribution of sample means based on samples of $n = 16$ selected from this population will have an expected value of $80/4 = 20$.

7. The standard error for a sample mean can never be larger than the standard deviation of the population from which the sample is selected.

8. A sample of $n = 25$ scores has a standard error of 2. This sample was selected from a population with $\sigma = 50$.

9. A researcher obtained $M = 27$ for a sample of $n = 36$ scores selected from a population with $\mu = 30$ and $\sigma = 12$. This sample mean corresponds to a z-score of $z = -1.50$.

10. Assuming that all other factors are held constant, as the population variability increases, the standard error will also increase.

Multiple-Choice Questions

1. The mean of the distribution of sample means is called _____.
    a. the expected value of M
    b. the standard error of M
    c. the sample mean
    d. the central limit mean

2. For a population with $\mu = 80$ and $\sigma = 20$, the distribution of sample means based on $n = 16$ will have an *expected value* of ____.
    a.   5
    b.   15
    c.   20
    d.   80

3. The distribution of sample means ____ .
    a. is always a normal distribution.
    b. will be normal *only if* the population distribution is normal.
    c. will be normal *only if* the sample size is at least $n = 30$.
    d. we be normal *if either* the population is normal or the sample size is $n \geq 30$.

4. If other factors are held constant, the expected value of M will _____ as the sample size increases.
    a. increase
    b. decrease
    c. stay constant
    d. cannot answer with the information given

5. A sample of $n = 25$ scores is selected from a population with $\mu = 100$ with $\sigma = 20$. On average, how much error would be expected between the sample mean and the population mean?
    a.   25 points
    b.   20 points
    c.   4 points
    d.   0.8 points

6. A sample of $n = 25$ scores is determined to have a standard error of 2 points. What is the standard deviation for the population from which the sample was obtained?
    a. 2
    b. 2/5
    c. 10
    d. 50

7. A random sample is selected from a population with a standard deviation of $\sigma = 20$. If the sample mean has a standard error of 2 points, how many scores are in the sample?
    a. $n = 5$
    b. $n = 10$
    c. $n = 25$
    d. $n = 100$

8. Which of the following samples would have the smallest standard error?
    a. $n = 25$ scores from a population with $\sigma = 10$
    b. $n = 25$ scores from a population with $\sigma = 20$
    c. $n = 100$ scores from a population with $\sigma = 10$
    d. $n = 100$ scores from a population with $\sigma = 20$

9. A normal population has $\mu = 50$ and $\sigma = 8$. A random sample of $n = 4$ scores from this population has a mean of 54. What is the z-score for this sample mean?
    a. +0.50
    b. +1.00
    c. +2.00
    d. +4.00

10. As sample size increases, the standard error of M _____.
    a. increases
    b. decreases
    c. stays constant

11. A sample of $n = 4$ scores from a specific population has a standard error of 8 points. For the same population, what would be the standard error for a sample of $n = 16$ scores?
    a. 1
    b. 2
    c. 4
    d. 8

12. A random sample of n = 4 scores is obtained from a population with σ = 10. If the sample mean is 10 points greater than the population mean, what is the z-score for the sample mean?
   a. +10.00
   b. +2.00
   c. +1.00
   d. cannot be determined without knowing the population mean

13. For a normal population with μ = 80 and σ = 20 which of the following samples is *least likely* to be obtained?
   a. M greater than 90 for a sample of n = 4
   b. M greater than 85 for a sample of n = 4
   c. M greater than 88 for a sample of n = 25
   d. M greater than 84 for a sample of n = 25

14. A sample of n = 4 scores is selected from a population with μ = 100 and σ = 20. If the sample mean is M = 110, what is the z-score for this sample mean?
   a. 0.50
   b. 1.00
   c. 2.00
   d. 4.00

15. A random sample of n = 4 scores is selected from a normally distributed population with μ = 80 and σ = 12. What is the probability that the sample mean will be greater than 86?
   a. 0.0228
   b. 0.0668
   c. 0.1587
   d. 0.3085

Other Questions

1. A population has a mean of μ = 100 and a standard deviation of σ = 10.
   a. If a single score is randomly selected from this population, how much distance, on average, should you find between the score and the population mean?
   b. If a sample of n = 4 scores is randomly selected from this population, how close on the average should the sample mean be to the population mean?
   c. If a sample of n = 100 scores is randomly selected from this population, how close on the average should the sample mean be to the population mean?

2. Each of the following samples was obtained from a population with $\mu = 100$ and $\sigma = 10$. Find the z-score for each sample mean.
     a. M = 90 for a sample of n = 4
     b. M = 90 for a sample of n = 25
     c. M = 102 for a sample of n = 4
     d. M = 102 for a sample of n = 100

3. For a normal population with $\mu = 70$ and $\sigma = 12$:
     a. What is the probability of obtaining a sample mean greater than 73 for a sample of n = 36 scores?
     b. What is the probability of obtaining a sample mean greater than 73 for a sample of n = 9 scores?

4. Given a normal population with $\mu = 40$ and $\sigma = 8$, what is the probability of obtaining a sample mean between 39 and 41 for a sample of n = 16 scores?

ANSWERS TO SELF TEST

True/False Answers

1. True
2. True
3. False. The mean is called the expected value of M.
4. False. With a sample size of n = 30 or more, the sample mean should be close to μ but probably not equal to μ.
5. False. The standard deviation is divided by the square root of n.
6. False. The expected value is $\mu = 80$.
7. True
8. False. The population standard deviation is 10.
9. True
10. True

Multiple-Choice Answers

1. a The average value of M is called the expected value.
2. d The expected value of M is always equal to μ.
3. d Either criterion is sufficient for a normal distribution.
4. c The expected value of M is equal to μ, independent of n.

5. c The standard error is $20/5 = 4$.
6. c The standard error is $10/5 = 2$.
7. d The standard error is $20/10 = 2$. $10 = \sqrt{100}$
8. c The smallest standard deviation and the biggest sample will produce the smallest error.
9. b With a mean of 50 and a standard error of 4, M = 54 corresponds to z = 1.00.
10. b The bigger the sample, the smaller the error.
11. c Standard error is declines by the square root of n. If the sample is 4 times larger, the error is reduced by 1/2.
12. b The standard error is $10/2 = 5$. Ten points is two standard errors.
13. c The largest sample with the most extreme mean will produce the most extreme z-score.
14. b With a mean of 100 and a standard error of 10, M = 110 corresponds to z = 1.00.
15. c With a mean of 80 and a standard error of 6, M = 86 corresponds to z = 1.00 which has 0.1587 in the tail.

Other Answers

1 a. The standard deviation, $\sigma = 10$, measures the standard distance between a score and the population mean.
   b. For n = 4, the standard error is $10/\sqrt{4} = 5$ points.
   c. For a sample of n = 100, the standard error is 1 point.

2 a. The standard error is 5, and z = -2.00.
   b. The standard error is 2, and z = -5.00.
   c. The standard error is 5, and z = +0.40.
   d. The standard error is 1, and z = +2.00.

3. a. The standard error is 2. $p(M > 73) = p(z > +1.50) = 0.0668$.
   b. The standard error is 4. $p(M > 73) = p(z < 0.75) = 0.2266$.

4. The standard error is 2. The probability is $p(-0.50 < z < +0.50) = 0.3830$. [2(.1915) using the value from Column D in the unit normal table]

CHAPTER 8

INTRODUCTION TO HYPOTHESIS TESTING

CHAPTER SUMMARY

The goals of Chapter 8 are:
1. To introduce the statistical technique of hypothesis testing.
2. To introduce the concepts of null hypothesis, alpha level, and critical region.
3. To introduce the types of errors that can occur in a hypothesis test.
4. To demonstrate the differences between one-tailed tests and two-tailed tests.
5. To introduce the concept of effect size as a supplement to a hypothesis test.
6. To introduce the concept of power for a hypothesis test.

Hypothesis Testing

The general goal of a hypothesis test is to rule out chance (sampling error) as a plausible explanation for the results from a research study. In this chapter, we introduced hypothesis testing as a technique to help determine whether a specific treatment has an effect on the individuals in a population. The hypothesis test is used to evaluate the results from a research study in which
1. A sample is selected from the population.
2. The treatment is administered to the sample.
3. After treatment, the individuals in the sample are measured.

If the individuals in the sample are noticeably different from the individuals in the original population, we have evidence that the treatment has an effect. However, it is also possible that the difference between the sample and the population is simply sampling error (see Figure 1.2 in your textbook). The purpose of the hypothesis test is to decide between two explanations:
1. The difference between the sample and the population can be explained by sampling error (there does not appear to be a treatment effect)
2. The difference between the sample and the population is too large to be explained by sampling error (there does appear to be a treatment effect).

The Null Hypothesis, the Alpha Level, the Critical Region, and the Test Statistic

The following four steps outline the process of hypothesis testing and introduce some of the new terminology.

1. State the hypotheses and select an α level. The **null hypothesis**, H_0, always states that the treatment has no effect (no change, no difference). According to the null hypothesis, the population mean after treatment is the same is it was before treatment. The **α level** establishes a criterion, or "cut-off", for making a decision about the null hypothesis. The alpha level also determines the risk of a Type I error.

2. Locate the critical region. The **critical region** consists of outcomes that are very unlikely to occur if the null hypothesis is true. That is, the critical region is defined by sample means that are almost impossible to obtain if the treatment has no effect. The phrase "almost impossible" means that these samples have a probability (p) that is less than the alpha level.

3. Compute the test statistic. The **test statistic** (in this chapter a z-score) forms a ratio comparing the obtained difference between the sample mean and the hypothesized population mean versus the amount of difference we would expect without any treatment effect (the standard error).

4. A large value for the test statistic shows that the obtained mean difference is more than would be expected if there is no treatment effect. If it is large enough to be in the critical region, we conclude that the difference is **significant** or that the treatment has a significant effect. In this case we reject the null hypothesis. If the mean difference is relatively small, then the test statistic will have a low value. In this case, we conclude that the evidence from the sample is not sufficient, and the decision is fail to reject the null hypothesis.

Errors in Hypothesis Tests

Conclusions from hypothesis tests can get a bit tricky. Just because the sample mean (following treatment) is different from the original population mean does not necessarily indicate that the treatment has caused a change. You should recall that there usually is some discrepancy between a sample mean and the population mean simply as a result of sampling error. This point was first demonstrated in Figure 1.2. Because the hypothesis test relies on sample data, and because sample data are not completely reliable, there is always the risk that misleading data will cause the hypothesis test to reach a wrong conclusion. Two types of error are possible:

1. A **Type I error** occurs when the sample data appear to show a treatment effect when, in fact, there is none. In this case the researcher will reject the null hypothesis and falsely conclude that the treatment has an effect. Type I errors are caused by unusual, unrepresentative samples. Just by chance the researcher selects an extreme sample with the result that the sample falls in the critical region even though the treatment has no effect. Fortunately, the hypothesis test is structured so that Type I errors are very unlikely; specifically, the probability of a Type I error is equal to the alpha level.

2. A **Type II error** occurs when the sample does not appear to have been affected by the treatment when, in fact, the treatment does have an effect. In this case, the researcher will fail to reject the null hypothesis and falsely conclude that the treatment does not have an effect. Type II errors are commonly the result of a very small treatment effect. Although the treatment does have an effect, it is not large enough to show up in the research study.

Directional Tests

When a research study predicts a specific direction for the treatment effect (increase or decrease), it is possible to incorporate the directional prediction into the hypothesis test. The result is called a **directional test** or a **one-tailed test**. A directional test includes the directional prediction in the statement of the hypotheses and in the location of the critical region. For example, if the original population has a mean of $\mu = 80$ and the treatment is predicted to increase the scores, then the null hypothesis would state that after treatment:

H_0: $\mu \leq 80$ (there is no increase)

In this case, the entire critical region would be located in the right-hand tail of the distribution because large values for M would demonstrate that there is an increase and would tend to reject the null hypothesis.

Measuring Effect Size

A hypothesis test evaluates the *statistical significance* of the results from a research study. That is, the test determines whether or not it is likely that the obtained sample mean occurred without any contribution from a treatment effect. As we demonstrated in Example 8.5 in the textbook (page 216), the hypothesis test is influenced not only by the size of the treatment effect but also by the size of the sample. Thus, even a very small effect can be significant if it is observed in a very large sample. Because a significant effect does not necessarily mean a large effect, it is recommended that the hypothesis test be accompanied by a measure of the **effect size**. In this chapter, we introduce Cohen's d as a standardized measure of effect size. Much like a z-score, **Cohen's d** measures the size of the mean difference in terms of the standard deviation.

Power of a Hypothesis Test

The **power** of a hypothesis test is defined is the probability that the test will reject the null hypothesis when the treatment does have an effect. The power of a test depends on a variety of factors including the size of the treatment effect and the size of the sample.

LEARNING OBJECTIVES

1. Understand the logic of hypothesis testing.

2. Be able to state the hypotheses and find the critical region.

3. Be able to assess sample data with a z-score and make a statistical decision about the hypotheses.

4. Understand the errors that can occur in a hypothesis test: Type I and Type II errors.

5. When an experiment contains a prediction about the direction of a treatment effect, you should be able to incorporate the directional prediction into the hypothesis testing procedure and conduct a directional (one-tailed) hypothesis test.

6. Understand why a measure of effect size should accompany a hypothesis and be able to compute Cohen's d and understand what it measures.

7. Understand the concept of power for a hypothesis test and recognize the factors that influence power.

NEW TERMS AND CONCEPTS

The following terms were introduced in Chapter 8. You should be able to define or describe each term and, where appropriate, describe how each term is related to other terms in the list.

hypothesis testing	A statistical procedure that uses data from a sample to test a hypothesis about a population.
null hypothesis, H_0	The null hypothesis states that there is no effect, no difference, or no relationship.

alternative hypothesis, H_1	The alternative hypothesis states that there is an effect, there is a difference, or there is a relationship.
Type I error	A Type I error is rejecting a true null hypothesis. You have concluded that a treatment does have an effect when actually it does not.
Type II error	A Type II error is failing to reject a false null hypothesis. The test fails to detect a real treatment effect.
alpha (α)	Alpha is a probability value that defines the *very unlikely* outcomes if the null hypothesis is true. Alpha also is the probability of committing a Type I error.
level of significance	The level of significance is the alpha level, which measures the probability of a Type I error.
critical region	The critical region consists of outcomes that are very unlikely to be obtained if the null hypothesis is true. The term *very unlikely* is defined by α.
test statistic	A statistic that summarizes the sample data in a hypothesis test. The test statistic is used to determine whether or not the data are in the critical region.
beta (β)	Beta is the probability of a Type II error.
directional (one-tailed) test	A directional test is a hypothesis test that includes a directional prediction in the statement of the hypotheses and places the critical region entirely in one tail of the distribution.
effect size	A measure of the size of the treatment effect that is separate from the statistical significance of the effect
power	The probability that the hypothesis test will reject the null hypothesis when there actually is a treatment effect.

NEW FORMULAS

$p(\text{Type I Error}) = \alpha$

$p(\text{Type II Error}) = \beta$

$$\text{Cohen's d} = \frac{\text{Mean Difference}}{\text{Standard Deviation}} = \frac{M - \mu}{\sigma}$$

STEP BY STEP

<u>Using a Sample to Test a Hypothesis about a Population Mean</u>: Although the hypothesis testing procedure is presented repeatedly in the textbook, we will demonstrate one more example here. As always, we will use the standard four-step procedure. The following generic example will be used for this demonstration.

The researcher begins with a known population, in this case a normal distribution with $\mu = 50$ and $\sigma = 10$. The researcher suspects that a particular treatment will produce a change in the scores for the individuals in the population. Because it is impossible to administer the treatment to the entire population, a sample of $n = 25$ individuals is selected and the treatment is given to the sample. After receiving the treatment, the average score for the sample is $M = 53$. Although the experiment involves only a sample, the researcher would like to use the data to make a general conclusion about how the treatment affects the entire population.

Step 1:   The first step is to state the hypotheses and select an alpha level. The hypotheses always concern an unknown population. For this example, the researcher does not know what would happen if the entire population were given the treatment. Nonetheless, it is possible to state hypotheses about the effect of the treatment. Specifically, the null hypothesis says that the treatment has no effect. According to H_0, the unknown population (after treatment) is identical to the original population (before treatment). In symbols,
   H_0: $\mu = 50$ (After treatment, the mean is still 50)

The alternative to the null hypothesis is that the treatment does have an effect that causes a change in the population mean. In symbols,
   H_1: $\mu \neq 50$ (After treatment, the mean is different from 50)

At this time you also select the alpha-level. Traditionally, α is set at .05 or .01. If there is particular concern about a Type I error, or if a researcher desires to present overwhelming evidence for a treatment effect, a smaller alpha-level can be used (such as $\alpha = .001$).

Step 2:   The next step is to locate the critical region. You should recall that the critical region is defined as the set of outcomes that are very unlikely to be obtained if the null hypothesis is true. We begin by looking at all the possible outcomes that could be obtained, then use the alpha level to determine the outcomes that are very unlikely. For this example, we look at the distribution of sample means for $n = 25$; that is, all the possible sample means that could be obtained if H_0 were true.

The distribution of sample means will be normal because the original population is normal. The expected value is $\mu = 50$ (if H_0 is true), and the standard error for $n = 25$ is

$$\sigma_M = \frac{\sigma}{\sqrt{n}} = \frac{10}{\sqrt{25}} = \frac{10}{5} = 2$$

With $\alpha = .05$, we want to identify the most unlikely 5% of this distribution. The boundaries for the extreme 5% are determined by z-scores of $z = \pm 1.96$.

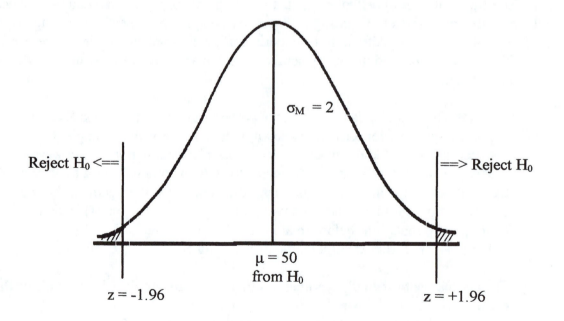

Step 3:   Obtain the Sample Data and Compute the Test Statistic. For this

example we obtained a sample mean of $M = 53$. This sample mean corresponds to a z-score of,

$$z = \frac{M - \mu}{\sigma_M} = \frac{53 - 50}{2} = \frac{3}{2} = 1.50$$

Step 4: Make Your Decision. The z-score we obtained is not in the critical region. This means that our sample mean, $M = 53$, is not an extreme or unusual value to be obtained from a population with $\mu = 50$. Therefore, we conclude that this sample does not provide sufficient evidence to conclude that the null hypothesis is wrong. Our statistical decision is to fail to reject H_0. The conclusion for the experiment is that the data do not indicate that the treatment has a significant effect. Note that the decision always consists of two parts:
1) a statistical decision about the null hypothesis, and
2) a conclusion about the outcome of the experiment

Measuring Effect Size with Cohen's d: Although effect size is more commonly measured after a hypothesis test in which H_0 is rejected, we will compute Cohen's d for the data from the preceding example. The original (untreated) population had $\mu = 50$. After treatment, the sample had a mean of $M = 53$, and the standard deviation was $\sigma = 10$. Using these values in the equation for Cohen's d, we obtain

$$\text{Cohen's d} = \frac{M - \mu}{\sigma} = \frac{53 - 50}{10} = 0.30$$

According to the criteria in Table 8.2, this is a small treatment effect.

HINTS AND CAUTIONS

1. When using samples with $n > 1$, we compute a z-score for the sample mean to determine if the sample data are unlikely. Be sure to use the standard error σ_M in the denominator, because the z-score is locating the sample mean within the distribution of sample means.

2. When stating the hypotheses for a directional test, remember that the predicted outcome (an increase or a decrease) is stated in the alternative hypothesis (H_1).

True/False Questions

1. In general, the null hypothesis states that the treatment has no effect on the population mean.

2. A Type II error occurs when you conclude that a treatment effect exists, but the treatment has no effect.

3. The *critical region* consists of extreme sample values that are very unlikely to occur if the null hypothesis is true.

4. If a specific sample leads to rejecting the null hypothesis with $\alpha = .01$, then the same sample would also lead to rejecting the null hypothesis with $\alpha = .05$.

5. One way to reduce the risk of a Type I error is to lower the alpha level.

6. If the obtained sample data are in the critical region, then we conclude that the data provide support for the null hypothesis.

7. In a research report, the term *statistically significant* is used to indicate that the null hypothesis was rejected.

8. In general, the larger the variance (or standard deviation), the more likely you are to reject the null hypothesis.

9. If a researcher is predicting that a treatment will produce an increase in scores, then the critical region for a directional test would be located entirely in the left-hand tail of the distribution.

10. Although the size of the sample can influence the outcome of a hypothesis test, it has little or no influence on measures of effect size.

Multiple-Choice Questions

1. By selecting a smaller alpha level, a researcher is _____.
    a. attempting to make it easier to reject H_0
    b. better able to detect a treatment effect
    c. reducing the risk of a Type I error
    d. All of the above

2. The critical boundaries for a hypothesis test are z = +1.96 and −1.96. If the z-score for the sample data is z = −1.90, then what is the correct statistical decision?
    a. Fail to reject H_1.
    b. Fail to reject H_0.
    c. Reject H_1.
    d. Reject H_0.

3. Increasing the alpha level (for example from α = .01 to α = .05) _____.
    a. increases the probability of a Type I error
    b. increases the size of the critical region
    c. increases the probability that the sample will fall into the critical region
    d. All of the above.

4. In a hypothesis test, an extreme z-score value, like z = +3 or z = +4, _____.
    a. is probably in the critical region
    b. means that you should probably reject the null hypothesis
    c. is strong evidence of a statistically significant effect
    d. All of the other options are correct.

5. In a hypothesis test, the critical region consist of
    a. sample values that are very unlikely to occur if the null hypothesis is true
    b. sample values that are very likely to occur if the null hypothesis is true
    c. sample values that are very unlikely to occur if the null hypothesis is false
    d. sample values that prove that the null hypothesis is true

6. A Type I error means that a researcher has _____.
    a. falsely concluded that a treatment has an effect
    b. correctly concluded that a treatment has no effect
    c. falsely concluded that a treatment has no effect
    d. correctly concluded that a treatment has an effect

7. A hypothesis test is used to evaluate the effect of a treatment. If the test decision is to reject the null hypothesis with α = .05, then _____.
    a. if the experiment were repeated, then there is a 95% chance that the same result would be obtained.
    b. if the experiment were repeated, then there is a 5% chance that the same result would be obtained.
    c. there is a 5% chance that the decision is wrong.
    d. there is a 95% chance that the decision is wrong.

8. A sample of n = 25 individuals is selected from a population with μ = 80 and a treatment is administered to the sample. If the treatment has no effect, then
    a. the sample mean should be very different from 80 and should lead you to reject the null hypothesis
    b. the sample mean should be very different from 80 and should lead you to fail to reject the null hypothesis
    c. the sample mean should be close to 80 and should lead you to reject the null hypothesis
    d. the sample mean should be close 80 and should lead you to fail to reject the null hypothesis

9. If a treatment has a very small effect, then a hypothesis test is likely to
    a. result in a Type I error.
    b. result in a Type II error.
    c. correctly reject the null hypothesis.
    d. correctly fail to reject the null hypothesis.

10. A population is known to have a mean of μ = 45. If a researcher predicts that the experimental treatment will produce a *decrease* in the scores, then the null hypothesis for a one-tailed test would state _____.
    a. $\mu \geq 45$
    b. $\mu \leq 45$
    c. $M \leq 45$
    d. $M \geq 45$

11. A researcher is conducting a hypothesis test to determine whether a treatment produces a significant increase in scores. If the sample data produce z = 1.89, which of the following conclusions is justified?
    a. Reject H_0 using a two-tailed test with σ = .05.
    b. Reject H_0 using a one-tailed test with σ = .05.
    c. Reject H_0 using a two-tailed test with σ = .01.
    d. Reject H_0 using a one-tailed test with σ = .01.

12. A researcher administers a treatment to a sample of n = 25 participants and uses a hypothesis test to evaluate the effect of the treatment. The hypothesis test produces a z-score of z = 2.77. Assuming that the researcher is using a two-tailed test,
    a. The researcher rejects the null hypothesis with σ = .05 but not with σ = .01.
    b. The researcher should reject the null hypothesis with either σ = .05 or σ = .01.
    c. The researcher should fail to reject H_0 with either σ = .05 or σ = .01.
    d. Cannot answer without additional information.

13. A treatment is administered to a sample selected from a population with a mean of $\mu = 80$ and a standard deviation of $\sigma = 10$. After treatment, the sample mean is M = 85. Based on this information, the effect size as measured by Cohen's d is _____.
    a. d = 5.00
    b. d = 2.00
    c. d = 0.50
    d. impossible to calculate without more information

14. A very small treatment effect can still be significant if
    a. the sample size (n) is very large.
    b. the sample standard deviation (σ) is very large
    c. the standard error of M (σ_M) is very large
    d. all of the above

15. Which of the following will increase the power of a hypothesis test?
    a. change α from .05 to .01
    b. change the sample size from 25 to 100
    c. change from a one-tailed test to a two-tailed test
    d. none of the other options will increase power

Other Questions

1. There is always some probability that a hypothesis test will lead to the wrong conclusion.
    a. Define a Type I error.
    b. Describe the consequences of a Type I error.
    c. What determines the probability of a Type I error.
    d. Define a Type II error.
    e. Describe the consequences of a Type II error.

2. Some researchers claim that herbal supplements such as ginseng or ginkgo biloba enhance human memory. To test this claim, a researcher selects a sample of n = 25 college students. Each student is given a ginkgo biloba supplement daily for six weeks and then all the participants are given a standardized memory test. Scores on the test are normally distributed with $\mu = 70$ and $\sigma = 15$. The sample of n = 25 students had a mean score of M = 75. Is this sample sufficient to conclude that the herb has a significant effect on memory? Use a two-tailed test with $\alpha = .05$.

3. A researcher would like to determine whether an over-the-counter cold medication has an effect on mental alertness. A sample of $n = 16$ participants is obtained, and each person is given a standard dose of the medication one hour before being tested in a driving simulation task. For the general population, reaction time scores on the simulation task are normally distributed with $\mu = 210$ and $\sigma = 20$. The individuals in the sample had an average score of $M = 222$.

      a. Can the research conclude that the medication has a significant effect on mental alertness as measured by the driving simulation task? Use a two-tailed test with $\alpha = .05$.

      b. Compute Cohen's d to measure the size of the effect.

ANSWERS TO SELF TEST

True/False Answers

1. True
2. False. A Type II error is concluding that there is no effect when there is.
3. True
4. True
5. True
6. False. With data in the critical region, the decision is to reject the null hypothesis.
7. True
8. False. Large variance lowers the likelihood of rejecting the null hypothesis.
9. False. Large scores (right-hand tail) indicate that the treatment works
10. True

Multiple-Choice Answers

1. c The alpha level is the probability of a Type I error. The smaller the alpha, the smaller the probability.
2. b The data are not in the critical region. Fail to reject the null hypothesis.
3. d Increasing alpha expands the critical region and increases the risk of a Type I error.
4. d The critical region is defined by extreme values.
5. a This is a definition of the *critical region*.
6. a A Type I error means that you conclude that the treatment has an effect, when it really does not.
7. c Alpha is the probability of a Type I error if H_0 is true.

8. d With no effect, the sample should be close to the hypothesized mean.
9. b If the treatment effect is very small, there is a good chance that the hypothesis test will fail to detect it (which is a Type II error).
10. a The null hypothesis says that there will be *no decrease*. (The mean is still 45, or even larger.)
11. b $z = 1.89$ is in the critical region only for a one-tailed test with $\alpha = .05$.
12. b The z-score exceeds the 1.96 value for .05 and the 2.58 value for .01.
13. c Cohen's d is the mean difference (5) divided by the standard deviation (10).
14. a With a very large sample, even a small effect can be significant.
15. b As sample size increases, so does the power of a test.

Other Answers

1. a. A Type I error is rejecting a true null hypothesis.
   b. With a Type I error, a researcher concludes that a treatment has an effect when in fact it does not. This can lead to a false report.
   c. The probability of a Type I error is the alpha level selected by the researcher.
   d. A Type II error is failing to reject a false null hypothesis.
   e. With a Type II error, a researcher concludes that the data do not provide a convincing demonstration that the treatment has any effect, when there is an effect. The researcher may choose to refine and repeat the experiment.

2. The critical region consists of values greater than $z = +1.96$ or less than $z = -1.96$. For this sample, the standard error is 3 and $z = 1.67$. Fail to reject the null hypothesis and conclude that this sample does not support the claim that the herb enhances memory.

3. a. The null hypothesis states that the medication has no effect: Stated in symbols, $H_0: \mu = 210$. The critical region consists of z-scores beyond 1.96 or -1.96. With a standard error of 5 points, the data produce a z-score of $z = 2.40$. Reject H_0 and conclude that medication has a significant effect on alertness.
   b. Cohen's $d = 12/20 = 0.60$, a medium effect according to the criteria in Table 8.2.

CHAPTER 9

INTRODUCTION TO THE t STATISTIC

CHAPTER SUMMARY

The goals of Chapter 9 are:
1. To introduce the t statistic as an alternative to the z-score hypothesis test.
2. To demonstrate the calculation of estimated standard error and the t statistic.
3. To introduce the t distributions and their relation to degrees of freedom.
4. To demonstrate the entire process of hypothesis testing with the t statistic.
5. To demonstrate the measurement of effect size for the t statistic.

The t Statistic

The t statistic introduced in Chapter 9 allows researchers to use sample data to test hypotheses about an unknown population mean. The particular advantage of the t statistic, compared to the z-score test in Chapter 8, is that the t statistic does not require any knowledge of the population standard deviation. Thus, the t statistic can be used to test hypotheses about a *completely unknown* population; that is, both μ and σ are unknown, and the only available information about the population comes from the sample. All that is required for a hypothesis test with t is a sample and a reasonable hypothesis about the population mean. There are two general situations where this type of hypothesis test is used:

1. The t statistic is used when a researcher wants to determine whether or not a treatment causes a change in a population mean. In this case you must know the value of μ for the original, untreated population. A sample is obtained from the population and the treatment is administered to the sample. If the resulting sample mean is significantly different from the original population mean, you can conclude that the treatment has a significant effect.

2. Occasionally a theory or other prediction will provide a hypothesized value for an unknown population mean. A sample is then obtained from the population and the t statistic is used to compare the actual sample mean with the hypothesized population mean. A significant difference indicates that the hypothesized value for μ should be rejected.

The Estimated Standard Error and the t Statistic

Whenever a sample is obtained from a population you expect to find some discrepancy or "error" between the sample mean and the population mean. This general phenomenon is known as **sampling error**, and was introduced in Figure 1.2 in your textbook. The goal for a hypothesis test is to evaluate the *significance* of the observed discrepancy between a sample mean and the population mean. Specifically, the hypothesis test attempts to decide between the following two alternatives:

1. Is it reasonable that the discrepancy between M and μ is simply due to sampling error and not the result of a treatment effect?
2. Is the discrepancy between M and μ more than would be expected by sampling error alone? That is, is the sample mean significantly different from the population mean?

The critical first step for the t statistic hypothesis test is to calculate exactly how much difference between M and μ is reasonable to expect. However, because the population standard deviation is unknown, it is impossible to compute the standard error of M as we did with z-scores in Chapter 8. Therefore, the t statistic requires that you use the sample data to compute an **estimated standard error of M**. This calculation defines standard error exactly as it was defined in Chapters 7 and 8, but now we must use the sample variance, s^2, in place of the unknown population variance, σ^2 (or use sample standard deviation, s, in place of the unknown population standard deviation, σ). The resulting formula for estimated standard error is

$$s_M = \sqrt{\frac{s^2}{n}} \qquad \text{or} \qquad s_M = \frac{s}{\sqrt{n}}$$

The t statistic (like the z-score) forms a ratio. The top of the ratio contains the obtained difference between the sample mean and the hypothesized population mean. The bottom of the ratio is the standard error which measures how much difference is expected by chance.

$$t = \frac{\text{obtained difference}}{\text{standard error}} = \frac{M - \mu}{s_M}$$

A large value for t (a large ratio) indicates that the obtained difference between the data and the hypothesis is greater than would be expected if the treatment has no effect.

The t Distributions and Degrees of Freedom

You should realize that the t statistic is very similar to the z-score used for hypothesis testing in Chapter 8. In fact, you can think of the t statistic as an "estimated z-score." The estimation comes from the fact that we are using the sample variance to estimate the unknown population variance. With a large sample, the estimation is very good and the t statistic will be very similar to a z-score. With small samples, however, the t statistic will provide a relatively poor estimate of z. The value of **degrees of freedom**, df = n - 1, is used to describe how well the t statistic represents a z-score. Also, the value of df will determine how well the distribution of t approximates a normal distribution. For large values of df, the **t distribution** will be nearly normal, but with small values for df, the t distribution will be flatter and more spread out than a normal distribution.

   To evaluate the t statistic from a hypothesis test, you must select an α level, find the value of df for the t statistic, and consult the t distribution table. If the obtained t statistic is larger than the critical value from the table, you can reject the null hypothesis. In this case, you have demonstrated that the obtained difference between the data and the hypothesis (numerator of the ratio) is significantly larger than the difference that would be expected if there was no treatment effect (the standard error in the denominator).

Hypothesis Tests with the t Statistic
   The hypothesis test with a t statistic follows the same four-step procedure that was used with z-score tests (Chapter 8):
  1. State the hypotheses and select a value for α. (Note: The null hypothesis always states a specific value for μ.)
  2. Locate the critical region.
   (Note: You must find the value for df and use the t distribution table.)
  3. Calculate the test statistic.
  4. Make a decision (Either "reject" or "fail to reject" the null hypothesis).

Measuring Effect Size with the t Statistic
   Because the significance of a treatment effect is determined partially by the size of the effect and partially by the size of the sample, you cannot assume that a significant effect is also a large effect. Therefore, it is recommended that a measure of effect size be computed along with the hypothesis test.

   For the t test it is possible to compute an estimate of Cohen's d just as we did for the z-score test in Chapter 8. The only change is that we now use the sample standard deviation instead of the population value (which is unknown).

$$\text{estimated Cohen's d} \;=\; \frac{\text{mean difference}}{\text{standard deviation}} \;=\; \frac{M - \mu}{s}$$

As before, Cohen's d measures the size of the treatment effect in terms of the standard deviation.

   With a t test it is also possible to measure effect size by computing the **percentage of variance accounted for** by the treatment. This measure is based on the idea that the treatment causes the scores to change, which contributes to the observed variability in the data. By measuring the amount of variability that can be attributed to the treatment, we obtain a measure of the size of the treatment effect. For the t statistic hypothesis test,

$$\text{percentage of variance accounted for} \; = \; r^2 \; = \; \frac{t^2}{t^2 + df}$$

LEARNING OBJECTIVES

1. Know when you must use the t statistic rather than a z-score for hypothesis testing.

2. Understand and be able to compute the estimated standard error and the t statistic for a sample mean.

3. Understand the concept of degrees of freedom and how it relates to the t distribution.

4. Be able to perform all of the necessary computations for hypothesis tests with the t statistic.

5. Be able to compute either an estimate of Cohen's d or the value for r^2 (the percentage of variance accounted for) to measure effect size for the t test.

NEW TERMS AND CONCEPTS

The following terms were introduced in this chapter. You should be able to define or describe each term and, where appropriate, describe how each term is related to other terms in the list.

t statistic

A statistic used to summarize sample data in situations where the population standard deviation is not known. The t statistic is similar to a z-score for a sample mean, but the t statistic uses an estimate of the standard error.

estimated standard error

An estimate of the standard error that uses the sample variance (or standard deviation) in place of the corresponding population value.

Chapter 9 - page 109

degrees of freedom (df)	Degrees of freedom = df = n - 1, measures the number of scores that are free to vary when computing SS for sample data. The value of df also describes how well a t statistic estimates a z-score.
t distribution	The distribution of t statistics is symmetrical and centered at zero like a normal distribution. A t distribution is flatter and more spread out than the normal distribution, but approaches a normal shape as df increases.
(r^2) the percentage of variance accounted for	A measure of effect size that determines what portion of the variability in the scores can be accounted for by the treatment effect.

NEW FORMULAS

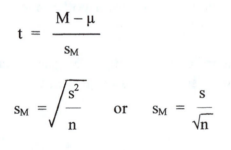

$$t = \frac{M - \mu}{s_M}$$

$$s_M = \sqrt{\frac{s^2}{n}} \quad \text{or} \quad s_M = \frac{s}{\sqrt{n}}$$

$$\text{percentage of variance accounted for} \ = \ r^2 \ = \ \frac{t^2}{t^2 + df}$$

STEP BY STEP

<u>Hypothesis Testing with the t Statistic</u>: The t statistic presented in this chapter is used to test a hypothesis about an unknown population mean using the data from a single sample. Calculation of the t statistic requires the sample mean M and some measure of the sample variability, usually the sample variance, s^2. A hypothesis test with the t statistic uses the same four-step procedure that we use for all hypothesis tests. However, with a t statistic, you must compute the variance (or standard deviation) for the sample of scores and you must remember to use the t distribution table to locate the critical values for the test. We will use the following example to demonstrate the t statistic hypothesis test.

A psychologist has prepared an "Optimism Test" that is administered yearly to graduating college seniors. The test measures how each graduating class feels about its future -- the higher the score, the more optimistic the class. Last year's class had a mean score of $\mu = 56$. A sample of $n = 25$ seniors from this year's class produced an average score of $M = 59$ with $SS = 2400$. On the basis of this sample can the psychologist conclude that this year's class has a different level of optimism than last year's class? Test at the .05 level of significance.

Note that this test will use a t statistic because the population standard deviation is not known.

Step 1: State Hypotheses and select an alpha level.
The statements of the null hypothesis and the alternative hypothesis are the same for the t statistic test as they were for the z-score test.

H_0: $\mu = 56$ (no change)
H_1: $\mu \neq 56$ (this year's mean is different)

For this example we are using $\alpha = .05$

Step 2: Locate the critical region. With a sample of $n = 25$, the t statistic will have $df = 24$. For a two-tailed test with $\alpha = .05$ and $df = 24$, the critical t values are $t = \pm 2.064$.

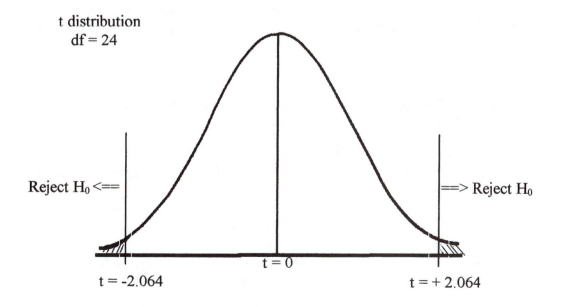

t distribution
df = 24

Reject H_0 <==   ==> Reject H_0

t = 0

t = -2.064   t = + 2.064

Step 3: Obtain the data and compute the test statistic: For this sample we have M = 59, SS = 2400, and n = 25. To compute the t statistic for these data, it is best to start by calculating the sample variance.

$$s^2 = \frac{SS}{n-1} = \frac{2400}{24} = 100$$

Next, use the sample variance to compute the estimated standard error. Remember, standard error provides a measure of the standard distance between a sample mean M and its population mean μ.

$$s_M = \sqrt{\frac{s^2}{n}} = \sqrt{\frac{100}{25}} = \sqrt{4} = 2$$

Finally, compute the t statistic using the hypothesized value of μ from H_0.

$$t = \frac{M - \mu}{s_M} = \frac{59 - 56}{2} = \frac{3}{2} = 1.50$$

Step 4: Make decision. The t statistic we obtained is not in the critical region. Because the sample mean is reasonably close to the hypothesized population mean, we fail to reject H_0. These data do not provide sufficient evidence to conclude that this year's graduating class has a level of optimism that is different from last year's class.

Measuring Effect Size for the t Statistic: Effect size can be measured by estimating Cohen's d or computing r^2. For the data from the hypothesis testing example,

$$\text{Cohen's d} = \frac{M - \mu}{s} = \frac{59 - 56}{10} = \frac{3}{10} = 0.30 \quad \text{(a small to medium effect)}$$

$$r^2 = \frac{t^2}{t^2 + df} = \frac{(1.50)^2}{(1.50)^2 + 24} = \frac{2.25}{26.25} = 0.086 \quad \text{(or 8.6\%)}$$

HINTS AND CAUTIONS

1. Students often confuse the formulas for sample variance (or standard deviation) and estimated standard error. The specific confusion is deciding when to divide by n and when to divide by n - 1.

Sample variance and standard deviation are *descriptive statistics* that were introduced in Chapter 4. You should recall that the sample mean describes the center of the distribution, and the sample standard deviation (or variance) describes how the scores are distributed around the mean. To compute the sample variance or the sample standard deviation, the correct denominator is df = n - 1.

The estimated standard error (s_M), on the other hand, is primarily an *inferential statistic* that measures how accurately the sample mean represents its population mean. The degree of accuracy is largely determined by the size of the sample: The bigger the sample, the smaller the error. Thus, the magnitude of the standard error is determined by n. To compute the estimated standard error, the correct denominator is n.

2. When locating the critical region for a t test, be sure to consult the t distribution table, not the unit normal table.

SELF TEST

True/False Questions

1. To calculate a t statistic, you must first compute the sample mean and the sample variance (or sample standard deviation).

2. The larger the value for df, the more a t distribution resembles a normal distribution.

3. In a t statistic, the estimated standard error provides a measure of how much difference is reasonable to expect between a sample mean and the population mean.

4. A sample of n = 25 scores with a sample variance of $s^2 = 100$ would have an estimated standard error of 4 points.

5. A researcher reports a t statistic with df = 30. This t statistic was computed for a sample of n = 29 scores.

6. As the value of df increases, the t distribution tends to become flatter and more spread out.

7. In a hypothesis test, a t statistic near zero indicates that the sample mean is relatively close to the population mean that is specified in the null hypothesis.

8. In a hypothesis test, the larger the value for the sample variance, the more likely it is that you will reject the null hypothesis.

9. For a two-tailed hypothesis test with $\alpha = .05$ and a sample of $n = 25$ scores, the boundaries for the critical region would be $t = \pm 2.060$.

10. Measures of effect size (such as Cohen's d and r^2) are relatively unaffected by the size of the sample.

Multiple-Choice Questions

1. In what circumstances is the t statistic used instead of a z-score for a hypothesis test?
   a. The t statistic is used when the sample size is $n = 30$ or larger.
   b. The t statistic is used when the population mean is unknown.
   c. The t statistic is used when the population variance (or standard deviation) is unknown.
   d. The t statistic is used if you are not sure that the population distribution is normal.

2. To calculate a t statistic, what information is needed from the sample?
   a. the value for n
   b. the value for M
   c. the value for s or s^2
   d. All of the other options are needed to compute t.

3. What is the estimated standard error for a sample of $n = 9$ scores with $s^2 = 36$?
   a. the square root of (36/9)
   b. the square root of (36/8)
   c. $36/\sqrt{9}$
   d. $36/\sqrt{8}$

4. The estimated standard error, s_M, provides a measure of the "average" or standard discrepancy between _____.
     a. a score and the population mean (X and μ)
     b. a sample mean and the population mean (M and μ)
     c. a score and the sample mean (X and M)
     d. None of the other options is correct.

5. Holding everything else constant, increasing sample size _____.
     a. decreases standard error
     b. increases the magnitude of the t statistic
     c. increases degrees of freedom
     d. All of the other options are consequences of increasing sample size.

6. With $\alpha = .05$ the two-tailed critical region for a sample of $n = 10$ participants would have boundaries of _____.
     a. $t = \pm 1.96$
     b. $t = \pm 1.833$
     c. $t = \pm 2.262$
     d. $t = \pm 2.228$

7. With $\alpha = .05$, the critical values for a two-tailed z-score test are ± 1.96. The corresponding values for a two-tailed t test with $\alpha = .05$ tend to be _____.
     a. less than ± 1.96 (closer to zero)
     b. greater than ± 1.96 (farther from zero)
     c. also equal to ± 1.96
     d. cannot be determined without additional information

8. As the sample size increases, what happens to the critical values for t? (Assume that the alpha level and all other factors remain constant.)
     a. the values increase
     b. the values decrease
     c. the values do not change when the sample size changes

9. A sample of $n = 15$ scores produces a t statistic of $t = -2.96$. If a researcher is using a regular two-tailed test with $\alpha = .01$, what decision should be made?
     a. reject the null hypothesis
     b. fail to reject the null hypothesis
     c. cannot determine without more information

10. A sample of $n = 9$ scores has a mean of $M = 46$ and a variance of $s^2 = 36$. What is the estimated standard error for this sample?
- a. 12
- b. 6
- c. 4
- d. 2

11. A sample of $n = 25$ scores has a mean of $M = 40$ and a variance of $s^2 = 100$. If this sample is being used to test a null hypothesis stating that $\mu = 43$, then what is the t statistic for the sample?
- a. $t = -3/20 = -0.15$
- b. $t = -0.30$
- c. $t = -3/4 = -0.75$
- d. $t = -3/2 = -1.50$

12. A researcher reports a t statistic with $df = 20$. Based on this information, how many individuals were in the sample?
- a. 19
- b. 20
- c. 21
- d. cannot be determined without more information

13. A sample of $n = 4$ individuals is obtained from a population with $\mu = 80$. Which set of sample statistics would produce the most extreme value for t?
- a. $M = 84$ and $s^2 = 8$
- b. $M = 84$ and $s^2 = 32$
- c. $M = 88$ and $s^2 = 8$
- d. $M = 88$ and $s^2 = 32$

14. A sample of $n = 25$ scores is obtained from a population with $\mu = 80$. Which of the following sets of sample statistics will produce the most extreme value for the t statistic?
- a. $M = 85$ with $s^2 = 10$
- b. $M = 90$ with $s^2 = 10$
- c. $M = 85$ with $s^2 = 100$
- d. $M = 90$ with $s^2 = 100$

15. A sample of $n = 16$ individuals is selected from a population with $\mu = 80$ and a treatment is administered to the sample. After treatment, the sample mean is $M = 84$ and the sample variance is $s^2 = 100$. If Cohen's d is used to measure effect size for this study, what value will be obtained for d?

    a. $4/2.5 = 1.60$
    b. 0.40
    c. 0.04
    d. cannot be determined without additional information

Other Questions

1. A research study reports $t(14) = 2.17$.
    a. How many individuals participated in the study? (How big was the sample?)
    b. Is this t statistic sufficient to reject the null hypothesis using a two-tailed test with $\alpha = .05$?

2. A researcher would like to evaluate the effect of a new reading program for second-grade students. For the past five years, a standardized test given at the end of second grade has produced a mean score of $\mu = 45$. A sample of $n = 25$ students is placed in the new program and, at the end of the school year they obtain a mean test score of $M = 51$ with $SS = 9600$. Based on these data can the researcher conclude that the new program has a significant effect on reading scores. Use a two-tailed test with $\alpha = .05$.
    a. Using symbols, state the hypotheses for this test.
    b. Locate the critical region for $\alpha = .05$.
    c. Calculate the t statistic for this sample.
    d. What decision should the researcher make?
    e. Compute Cohen's d and r^2 to measure the size of the effect.

3. A researcher obtains the following sample from a population with an unknown mean and unknown standard deviation.
    Sample: 5, 0, 4, 7, 3, 7, 8, 2, 9
    a. Compute the mean, variance, and standard deviation for the sample.
    b. Use the sample variance to compute the estimated standard error, s_M, for the sample mean.
    c. Use the sample to test the null hypothesis that the population mean is equal to $\mu = 8$. Use a two-tailed test with $\alpha = .05$. (Assume the population distribution is normal.)

ANSWERS TO SELF TEST

True/False Answers

1. True
2. True
3. True
4. False. The estimated standard error is the square root of 4.
5. False. A sample of $n = 31$ would have $df = 30$.
6. False. As df increases, the t distribution becomes taller and more compact like a normal shaped distribution.
7. True
8. False. The larger the sample variance, the less likely it is that you will reject the null hypothesis.
9. False. With $df = 24$, the critical values are ± 2.064.
10. True

Multiple-Choice Answers

1. c The t statistic uses the sample variance to estimate the unknown population value.
2. d The t statistic requires the sample variance as well as M and n.
3. a Estimated standard error equals the square root of (s^2/n).
4. b The estimated standard error measures the standard distance between M and μ.
5. d Increasing n decreases the error in the denominator of the t statistic.
6. c With $df = 9$ and .05 in two tails combined, $t = \pm 2.262$.
7. b Especially when n is small, t statistics are more variable than z-scores and form a flatter, more spread out distribution.
8. b As df increases, the t distribution becomes less spread out.
9. b With $df = 14$ and $\alpha = .01$, the critical value is 2.977.
10. d Estimated standard error equals the square root of (s^2/n).
11. d The estimated standard error is 2, and $t = -3/2$.
12. c $df = n - 1$
13. c The most extreme sample has the biggest mean difference and the smallest variance.
14. b The most extreme sample has the biggest mean difference and the smallest variance.
15. b The sample standard deviation is 10, and Cohen's $d = 4/10$.

1. a. With $df = 14$, the sample size is $n = 15$,
    b. With $df = 14$, the critical values are $t = \pm 2.145$.   Reject H_0.

2. a. H_0: $\mu = 45$ and H_1: $\mu \neq 45$
    b. With $df = 24$, the critical values are $t = \pm 2.064$.
    c. The sample variance is $s^2 = 400$, the standard error is 4, and $t = 1.50$.
    d. Fail to reject H_0. The data indicate that the new program does not have a significant effect on reading scores.
    e. Cohen's $d = 6/\sqrt{400} = 0.30$. The percentage of variance accounted for is $r^2 = 2.25/(2.25 + 24) = 0.086$ (or 8.6%).

3. a. $M = 5$, $s^2 = 9$, and $s = 3$
    b. The estimated standard error is 1 point.
    c. If $\mu = 8$ (from H_0), then $t = 3.00$. This is beyond the critical value of 2.306 so the decision is to reject the null hypothesis.

CHAPTER 10

THE t TEST FOR
TWO INDEPENDENT SAMPLES

CHAPTER SUMMARY

The goals of Chapter 10 are:
1. To introduce the basic characteristics of an independent-measures (or between-subjects) research design.
2. To demonstrate the process of hypothesis testing with the independent-measures t statistic.
3. To introduce the assumption of homogeneity of variance.
4. To demonstrate the measurement of effect size for the independent-measures t.

Independent-Measures Designs
    The independent-measures hypothesis test allows researchers to evaluate the mean difference between two populations using the data from two separate samples. The identifying characteristic of the **independent-measures** or **between-subjects** design is the existence of two separate or independent samples. Thus, an independent-measures design can be used to test for mean differences between two distinct populations (such as men versus women) or between two different treatment conditions (such as drug versus no-drug). The independent-measures design is used in situations where a researcher has no prior knowledge about either of the two populations (or treatments) being compared. In particular, the population means and standard deviations are all unknown. Because the population variances are not known, these values must be estimated from the sample data.

Hypothesis Testing with the Independent-Measures t Statistic
    As with all hypothesis tests, the general purpose of the independent-measures t test is to determine whether the sample mean difference obtained in a research study indicates a real mean difference between the two populations (or treatments) or whether the

obtained difference is simply the result of sampling error. Remember, if two samples are taken from the same population and are given exactly the same treatment, there still will be some difference between the sample means. This difference is called sampling error (see Figure 1.2 in your textbook). The hypothesis test provides a standardized, formal procedure for determining whether the mean difference obtained in a research study is significantly greater than can be explained by sampling error.

To prepare the data for analysis, the first step is to compute the sample mean and SS (or s, or s^2) for each of the two samples. The hypothesis test follows the same four-step procedure outlined in Chapters 8 and 9.

1. State the hypotheses and select an α level. For the independent-measures test, H_0 states that there is no difference between the two population means.

2. Locate the critical region. The critical values for the t statistic are obtained using degrees of freedom that are determined by adding together the df value for the first sample and the df value for the second sample.

3. Compute the test statistic. The t statistic for the independent-measures design has the same structure as the single sample t introduced in Chapter 9. However, in the independent-measures situation, all components of the t formula are doubled: there are two sample means, two population means, and two sources of error contributing to the standard error in the denominator.

4. Make a decision. If the t statistic ratio indicates that the obtained difference between sample means (numerator) is substantially greater than the difference expected by chance (denominator), we reject H_0 and conclude that there is a real mean difference between the two populations or treatments.

The Homogeneity of Variance Assumption

Although most hypothesis tests are built on a set of underlying assumptions, the tests usually work reasonably well even if the assumptions are violated. The one notable exception is the assumption of **homogeneity of variance** for the independent-measures t test. The assumption requires that the two populations from which the samples are obtained have equal variances. This assumption is necessary in order to justify pooling the two sample variances and using the pooled variance in the calculation of the t statistic. If the assumption is violated, then the t statistic contains two questionable values: (1) the value for the population mean difference which comes from the null hypothesis, and (2) the value for the pooled variance. The problem is that you cannot determine which of these two values is responsible for a t statistic that falls in the critical region. In particular, you cannot be certain that rejecting the null hypothesis is correct when you obtain an extreme value for t. If the two sample variances appear to be substantially different, you should use Hartley's F-max test to determine whether or not the homogeneity assumption is satisfied. If homogeneity of variance is violated, Box 10.3 presents an alternative procedure for computing the t statistic that does not involve pooling the two sample variances.

Measuring Effect Size for the Independent-Measures t

Effect size for the independent-measures t is measured in the same way that we measured effect size for the single-sample t in Chapter 9. Specifically, you can compute an estimate of Cohen's d or you can compute r^2 to obtain a measure of the percentage of variance accounted for by the treatment effect.

LEARNING OBJECTIVES

1. You should be able to describe and to recognize the experimental situations for which an independent-measures t statistic is appropriate.

2. You should be able to use the independent-measures t statistic to test hypotheses about the mean difference between two populations (or between two treatment conditions).

3. You should be able to list the assumptions that must be satisfied before an independent-measures t statistic can be computed or interpreted.

4. You should be able to use the sample data to compute r^2 or an estimate of Cohen's d to measure effect size for the independent-measures t.

NEW TERMS AND CONCEPTS

The following terms were introduced in Chapter 10. You should be able to define or describe each term and, where appropriate, describe how each term is related to others in the list.

independent-measures design	A research design that uses a separate sample for each treatment condition or each population being compared.
between-subjects design	An alternative term for an independent-measures design.

repeated-measures design	A research design that uses the same group of subjects in all of the treatment conditions that are being compared.
within-subjects design	An alternative term for a repeated-measures design.
pooled variance	A single measure of sample variance that is obtained by averaging two sample variances. It is a weighted mean of the two variances.
homogeneity of variance	An assumption that the two populations from which the samples were obtained have equal variances.

NEW FORMULAS

$$t = \frac{(M_1 - M_2) - (\mu_1 - \mu_2)}{s_{M_1 - M_2}}$$

$$df = (n_1 - 1) + (n_2 - 1)$$
$$= n_1 + n_2 - 2$$

$$s_{M_1 - M_2} = \sqrt{\frac{s_P^2}{n_1} + \frac{s_P^2}{n_2}}$$

$$s_P^2 = \frac{SS_1 + SS_2}{df_1 + df_2}$$

$$F_{max} = \frac{s^2 \, (\text{largest})}{s^2 \, (\text{smallest})}$$

$$\text{estimated Cohen's d} = \frac{M_1 - M_2}{\sqrt{s_P^2}}$$

STEP BY STEP

Hypothesis Tests with the Independent-Measures t Statistic. The independent-measures t statistic is used in situations where a researcher wants to test a hypothesis about the difference between two population means using the data from two separate (independent) samples. The test requires both sample means (M_1 and M_2), and some measure of the variability for each sample (usually SS). The following example will be used to demonstrate the independent-measures t hypothesis test.

   A researcher wants to assess the damage to memory that is caused by excessive alcohol consumption. A sample of $n = 10$ adults with chronic alcoholism is obtained from a hospital treatment ward, and a control group of $n = 10$ non-drinkers is obtained from the hospital maintenance staff. Each person is given a brief memory test and the researcher records the memory score for each subject. The data are summarized as follows:

Alcoholism	Control
M = 43	M = 57
SS = 400	SS = 410

Step 1: State the hypotheses and select an alpha level. As always, the null hypothesis states that there is no effect.

   H_0: $(\mu_1 - \mu_2) = 0$ (no difference)

The alternative hypothesis says that there is a difference between the two population means.

   H_1: $(\mu_1 - \mu_2) \neq 0$

We will use $\alpha = .05$.

Step 2: Locate the critical region. With $n = 10$ in each sample, the t statistic will have degrees of freedom equal to, $df = (n_1 - 1) + (n_2 - 1) = 9 + 9 = 18$

   Sketch the entire distribution of t statistics with $df = 18$ and locate the extreme 5%. The critical values are $t = \pm 2.101$.

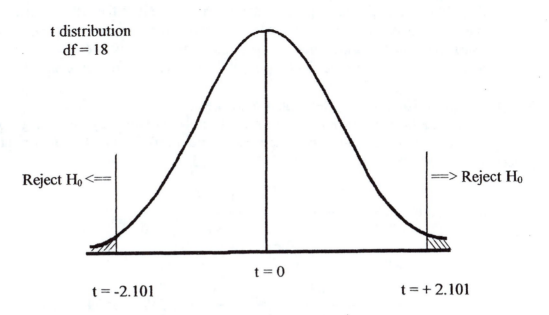

t distribution
df = 18

Reject H$_0$ <==   ==> Reject H$_0$

t = 0

t = -2.101   t = + 2.101

Step 3: Compute the t statistic. It is easiest to begin by computing the pooled variance for the two samples.

$$s_P^2 = \frac{SS_1 + SS_2}{df_1 + df_2} = \frac{400 + 410}{9 + 9} = \frac{810}{18} = 45$$

Next, calculate the standard error for the t statistic.

$$s_{M_1 - M_2} = \sqrt{\frac{s_P^2}{n_1} + \frac{s_P^2}{n_2}} = \sqrt{\frac{45}{10} + \frac{45}{10}}$$

$$= \sqrt{4.5 + 4.5}$$

$$= \sqrt{9} = 3$$

Finally, use the two sample means and the standard error to calculate the t statistic.

$$t = \frac{(M_1 - M_2) - (\mu_1 - \mu_2)}{s_{M_1 - M_2}} = \frac{(43 - 57) - 0}{3} = \frac{-14}{3} = -4.67$$

Step 4: Make decision. The t statistic for these data is in the critical region. This is a very unlikely outcome ($p < .05$) if H_0 is true, therefore, we reject H_0. The researcher concludes that there is a significant difference between the mean memory score for chronic alcoholics and the mean score for non-drinkers.

Measuring Effect Size for the Independent-Measures t

Effect size for the independent-measures t can be measured by estimating Cohen's d or computing r^2 (the percentage of variance accounted for). Using the data from the preceding example, these two measures are computed as follows:

$$\text{estimated Cohen's d} = \frac{M_1 - M_2}{\sqrt{s_P^2}} = \frac{43 - 57}{\sqrt{45}} = \frac{14}{6.71} = 2.09$$

$$r^2 = \frac{t^2}{t^2 + df} = \frac{(-4.67)^2}{(-4.67)^2 + 18} = \frac{21.81}{39.81} = 0.548 \quad (\text{or } 54.8\%)$$

HINTS AND CAUTIONS

1. One of the most common errors in computing the independent-measures t statistic occurs when students confuse the formulas for pooled variance and standard error. To compute the pooled variance, you combine the two samples into a single estimated variance. The formula for pooled variance uses a single fraction with the SS values in the numerator and the df values in the denominator:

$$s_P^2 = \frac{SS_1 + SS_2}{df_1 + df_2}$$

To compute the standard error, you add the separate errors for the two samples. In the formula for standard error these two separate sources of error appear as two separate fractions:

$$s_{M_1 - M_2} = \sqrt{\frac{s_P^2}{n_1} + \frac{s_P^2}{n_2}}$$

SELF TEST

True/False Questions

1. The null hypothesis for an independent-measures t test states that the two sample means are equal.

2. Two separate samples, each with n = 9, will produce an independent-measures t statistic with df = 16.

3. If two samples each have n = 5 and SS = 40, then the pooled variance is 10.

4. A researcher reports an independent-measures t statistic with df = 20. Based on the df value, you can conclude that the study used a total of 21 participants.

5. One sample has n = 8 scores and SS = 40. A second sample has n = 4 scores and SS = 20. The pooled variance for these two samples is 60/10 = 6.

6. For an independent-measures t statistic, the magnitude of the estimated standard error is inversely related to the size of the samples (the bigger the samples, the smaller the error).

7. The larger the values for the two sample variances, the greater the likelihood that the independent-measures t test will find a significant difference. (Assume all other factors are held constant.)

8. For a hypothesis test with an independent-measures t, the larger the difference between the two sample means, the greater the likelihood that you will reject the null hypothesis.

9. *Homogeneity of variance* assumes that the two population variances are equal.

10. Cohen's d is computed by first finding the difference between the two sample means and then dividing by the pooled variance.

Multiple-Choice Questions

1. Which of the following research situations would be most likely to use an independent-measures design?
   a. Examine the development of vocabulary as a group of children mature from age 2 to age 3.
   b. Examine the long-term effectiveness of a stop-smoking treatment by interviewing subjects 2 months and 6 months after the treatment ends.
   c. Compare the mathematics skills for 9th grade boys versus 9th grade girls.
   d. Compare the blood-pressure readings before medication and after medication for a group a patients with high blood pressure.

2. A researcher is comparing two treatment conditions with a sample of $n = 10$ in one treatment and a separate sample of $n = 15$ in the other. If the data are evaluated with an independent-measures t statistic, what is the df value for the statistic?
   a. 23
   b. 24
   c. 26
   d. 27

3. A researcher reports an independent-measures t statistic with df = 20. What is the total number of subjects who participated in the research study?
   a. 18
   b. 19
   c. 21
   d. 22

4. One sample of $n = 10$ scores has a variance of $s^2 = 10$ and a second sample of $n = 10$ scores has $s^2 = 20$. If the pooled variance is computed for these two samples, then the value obtained will be _____.
   a. closer to 10 than to 20
   b. closer to 20 than to 10
   c. exactly half way between 10 and 20
   d. cannot be determined without more information

5. One sample has n = 25 scores and a second sample has n = 15 scores. If the pooled variance is computed for the two samples, then the value for the pooled variance will be
    a. half-way between the two sample variances.
    b. between the two sample variances, but closer to the variance of the larger sample.
    c. between the two sample variances, but closer to the variance of the smaller sample.
    d. larger than either of the two sample variances.

6. What is the pooled variance for the following two samples?
    Sample 1: n = 6 and SS = 56
    Sample 2: n = 4 and SS = 40
    a. 5
    b. $\sqrt{5}$
    c. 12
    d. 9.6

7. What is the estimated standard error for the independent-measures t statistic for the following two samples?
    Sample 1: n = 6 and SS = 56
    Sample 2: n = 4 and SS = 40
    a. 5
    b. $\sqrt{5}$
    c. $\sqrt{2} + \sqrt{3}$
    d. $\sqrt{24/10}$

8. As the sample variance increases, the value of the t statistic _____.
    a. increases (moves away from zero)
    b. decreases (moves toward zero)
    c. approximates the value of $M_1 - M_2$
    d. the value of t is not influenced by sample variance

9. The null hypothesis for the independent-measures t test states _____.
    a. there is no difference between the two sample mean
    b. there is no difference between the two population means
    c. the difference between the two sample means is identical to the difference between the two population means
    d. None of the other 3 choices is correct.

10. Which of the following sets of data would produce the largest value for an independent-measures t statistic?

     a. The two sample means are 10 and 12 with sample variances of 20 and 25.
     b. The two sample means are 10 and 12 with variances of 120 and 125.
     c. The two sample means are 10 and 20 with variances of 20 and 25.
     d. The two sample means are 10 and 20 with variances of 120 and 125.

11. Which set of sample characteristics is most likely to produce a significant difference for an independent-measures t test?

     a. a large sample mean difference and large sample variances
     b. a large sample mean difference and small sample variances
     c. a small sample mean difference and large sample variances
     d. a small sample mean difference and small sample variances

12. In an independent-measures t hypothesis test, how does the magnitude for sample variance influence the size of the t statistic?

     a. The larger the sample variance, the larger the t value (farther from zero)
     b. The larger the sample variance, the smaller the t value (closer to zero)
     c. The magnitude of the sample variance has no influence on the t value.

13. In an independent-measures t hypothesis test, how is the t statistic related to the amount of difference between the two sample means?

     a. The larger the difference between means, the larger the value for t (farther from zero).
     b. The larger the difference between means, the smaller the value for t (closer to zero).
     c The magnitude of the t statistic is not related to the mean difference between samples.

14. The homogeneity of variance assumption states that _____.

     a. the two sample variances are equal
     b. the two samples come from the same population
     c. variance must stay constant for each subject in the experiment
     d. the samples come from populations with equal variances

15. For an independent-measures research study, one sample has $M = 20$ with $s = 22$ and the second sample has $M = 17$ with $s = 28$. The pooled variance is 25. What is the estimated value of Cohen's d for these data?

    a. $d = 3/25$

    b. $d = 3/8$

    c. $d = 3/5$

    d. The value of d cannot be determined without knowing the sample sizes.

Other Questions

1. A researcher would like to demonstrate how different schedules of reinforcement can influence behavior. Two separate groups of rats are trained to press a bar in order to receive a food pellet. One group is trained using a fixed ratio schedule where they receive one pellet for every 10 presses of the bar. The second group is trained using a fixed interval schedule where they receive one pellet for the first bar press that occurs within a 30 second interval. Note that the second group must wait 30 seconds before another pellet is possible no matter how many times the bar is pressed. After 4 days of training, the researcher records the response rate (number of presses per minute) for each rat. The results are summarized as follows:

Fixed Ratio	Fixed Interval
$n = 4$	$n = 8$
$M = 30$	$M = 18$
$SS = 90$	$SS = 150$

    a. Do these data indicate that there is a significant difference in responding for these two reinforcement schedules? Test at the .05 level of significance.

    b. Compute Cohen's d and r^2 to measure the size of the effect.

2. A psychologist is examining the influence of an older sibling in the development of social skills. A sample of 24 three-year-old children is obtained. Half of these children had no siblings and the others had at least one older sibling who is within 5 years of the child's age. The psychologist records a social skills score for each child and obtained the following data:

No Sibling	Older Sibling
$n = 12$	$n = 12$
$M = 17$	$M = 24$
$SS = 580$	$SS = 608$

Do these data indicate that having an older sibling has a significant effect on the development of social skills? Use a two-tailed test at the .05 level.

3. The following data are from two separate samples. Does it appear that these two samples came from the same population or from two different populations?
  a. Use an F-max test to determine whether there is evidence for a significant difference between the two population variances. Use the .05 level of significance.
  b. Use an independent-measures t test to determine whether there is evidence for a significant difference between the two population means. Again, use $\alpha = .05$.

Sample 1	Sample 2
n = 10	n = 10
M = 32	M = 18
SS = 890	SS = 550

ANSWERS TO SELF TEST

True/False Answers

1. False. The null hypothesis states that the two population means are equal.
2. True
3. True
4. False. The study used a total of 22 participants.
5. True
6. True
7. False. Increases in variance produce a smaller value for t (nearer to zero).
8. True
9. True
10. False. The mean difference is divided by the square root of the pooled variance.

Multiple-Choice Answers

1. c Comparing boys and girls would require two separate samples.
2. a The t statistic has df = $(n_1 - 1) + (n_2 - 1)$.
3. d The t statistic has df = $(n_1 - 1) + (n_2 - 1)$.
4. c If the two samples are the same size, the pooled variance is the average of the two sample variances.
5. b The larger sample carries more weight when computing pooled variance.

6. c   Pooled variance equals $(SS_1 + SS_2)/(df_1 + df_2)$
7. b   When computing standard error, you divide pooled variance by n for each sample, add the two values, and take the square root.
8. b   Increases in variance produce increases in the standard error and a smaller value for t (nearer to zero).
9. b   The null hypothesis always refers to the populations, not the samples.
10. c   The greatest difference between samples occurs with a big mean difference and small variances.
11. b   The greatest difference between samples occurs with a big mean difference and small variances.
12. b   The larger the variance, the larger the standard error and the smaller the t value.
13. a   The greatest difference between samples occurs with a big mean difference.
14. d   Homogeneity requires that the two populations have the same variance.
15. c   The standard deviation is estimated with the square root of the pooled variance. Cohen's d is the mean differences divided by the standard deviation.

Other Answers

1. a. With $df = 10$, the critical t values are $t = \pm 2.228$. These data have a pooled variance of 24 and produce a t statistic of $t = 4.00$. Reject H_0. The data provide sufficient evidence to conclude that there is a significant difference between the two schedules.
   b. Cohen's $d = 12/\sqrt{24} = 2.45$ and $r = 16/(16 + 10) = 0.615$ (or 61.5%)

2. The hypotheses are,
   H_0: $(\mu_1 - \mu_2) = 0$ (sibling has no effect)
   H_1: $(\mu_1 - \mu_2) \neq 0$ (sibling does have an effect)
   With $df = 22$, the critical region consists of t values beyond $t = \pm 2.074$. For these data, the pooled variance is 54, and $t = 2.33$. Reject H_0 and conclude that the children with siblings have significantly different social skills scores than those without siblings.

3. a. For these data, F-max $= 1.62$. The critical value for $\alpha = .05$ is 4.03. Fail to reject H_0. There is insufficient evidence to conclude that the two population variances are different.
   b. For these data the pooled variance is 80 and the t statistic is $t = 14/4 = 3.50$. Reject H_0 and conclude that the two population means are different.

CHAPTER 11

THE t TEST FOR TWO RELATED SAMPLES

CHAPTER SUMMARY

The goals of Chapter 11 are:

1. To introduce the basic characteristics of a repeated-measures (or within-subjects) research design.
2. To demonstrate the process of hypothesis testing with the repeated-measures t statistic.
3. To demonstrate the measurement of effect size for the repeated-measures t
4. To discuss the advantages and the disadvantages of a repeated-measures design compared to an independent-measures design.

Repeated-Measures Designs

The related-samples hypothesis test allows researchers to evaluate the mean difference between two treatment conditions using the data from a single sample. In a **repeated-measures design**, a single group of individuals is obtained and each individual is measured in both of the treatment conditions being compared. Thus, the data consist of two scores for each individual.

Hypothesis Tests with the Repeated-Measures t

The repeated-measures t statistic allows researchers to test a hypothesis about the population mean difference between two treatment conditions using sample data from a repeated-measures research study. In this situation it is possible to compute a **difference score** for each individual:

$$\text{difference score} = D = X_2 - X_1$$

Where X_1 is the person's score in the first treatment and X_2 is the score in the second treatment.

Note: The related-samples t test can also be used for a similar design, called a **matched-subjects design**, in which each individual in one treatment is matched one-to-one with a corresponding individual in the second treatment. The matching is accomplished by selecting pairs of subjects so that the two subjects in each pair have identical (or nearly identical) scores on the variable that is being used for matching. Thus, the data consist of pairs of scores with each pair corresponding to a matched set of two "identical" subjects. For a matched-subjects design, a difference score is computed for each matched pair of individuals. However, because the matching process can never be perfect, matched-subjects designs are relatively rare. As a result, repeated-measures designs (using the same individuals in both treatments) make up the vast majority of related-samples studies and we will focus on them.

The sample of difference scores is used to test hypotheses about the population of difference scores. The null hypothesis states that the population of difference scores has a mean of zero,

$$H_0: \mu_D = 0$$

In words, the null hypothesis says that there is no consistent or systematic difference between the two treatment conditions. Note that the null hypothesis does not say that each individual will have a difference score equal to zero. Some individuals will show a positive change from one treatment to the other, and some will show a negative change. On average, however, the entire population will show a mean difference of zero. Thus, according to the null hypothesis, the sample mean difference should be near to zero. Remember, the concept of sampling error states that samples are not perfect and we should always expect small differences between a sample mean and the population mean.

The alternative hypothesis states that there is a systematic difference between treatments that causes the difference scores to be consistently positive (or negative) and produces a non-zero mean difference between the treatments:

$$H_1: \mu_D \neq 0$$

According to the alternative hypothesis, the sample mean difference obtained in the research study is a reflection of the true mean difference that exists in the population.

The repeated-measures t statistic forms a ratio with exactly the same structure as the single-sample t statistic presented in Chapter 9. The numerator of the t statistic measures the difference between the sample mean and the hypothesized population mean. The bottom of the ratio is the standard error, which measures how much difference is reasonable to expect between a sample mean and the population mean if there is no treatment effect; that is, how much difference is expected by simply by sampling error.

$$t = \frac{\text{obtained difference}}{\text{standard error}} = \frac{M_D - \mu_D}{s_{M_D}} \qquad df = n - 1$$

For the repeated-measures t statistic, all calculations are done with the sample of difference scores. The mean for the sample appears in the numerator of the t statistic and the variance of the difference scores is used to compute the standard error in the denominator. As usual, the standard error is computed by

$$s_{M_D} = \sqrt{\frac{s^2}{n}} \qquad \text{or} \qquad s_{M_D} = \frac{s}{\sqrt{n}}$$

Measuring Effect Size for the Independent-Measures t

Effect size for the independent-measures t is measured in the same way that we measured effect size for the single-sample t (Chapter 9) and the independent-measures t (Chapter 10). Specifically, you can compute an estimate of Cohen's d to obtain a standardized measure of the mean difference, or you can compute r^2 to obtain a measure of the percentage of variance accounted for by the treatment effect.

Comparing Repeated-Measures and Independent-Measures Designs

Because a repeated-measures design uses the same individuals in both treatment conditions, this type of design usually requires fewer participants than would be needed for an independent-measures design. In addition, the repeated-measures design is particularly well suited for examining changes that occur over time, such as learning or development. The primary advantage of a repeated-measures design, however, is that it reduces variance and error by removing individual differences.

The first step in the calculation of the repeated-measures t statistic is to find the difference score for each subject. This simple process has two very important consequences.

1. First, the D score for each subject provides an indication of how much difference there is between the two treatments. If all of the subjects show roughly the same D scores, then you can conclude that there appears to be a consistent, systematic difference between the two treatments. You should also note that when all the D scores are similar, the variance of the D scores will be small, which means that the standard error will be small and the t statistic is more likely to be significant.

2. Also, you should note that the process of subtracting to obtain the D scores removes the individual differences from the data. That is, the initial differences

in performance from one subject to another are eliminated. Removing individual differences also tends to reduce the variance, which creates a smaller standard error and increases the likelihood of a significant t statistic.

The following data demonstrate these points.

Subject	X_1	X_2	D
A	9	16	7
B	25	28	3
C	31	36	5
D	58	61	3
E	72	79	7

First, notice that all of the subjects show an increase of roughly 5 points when they move from treatment 1 to treatment 2. Because the treatment difference is very consistent, the D scores are all clustered close together will produce a very small value for s^2. This means that the standard error in the bottom of the t statistic will be very small.

Second, notice that the original data show big differences from one subject to another. For example, subject B has scores in the 20's and subject E has scores in the 70's. However, these big **individual differences** are eliminated when the difference scores are calculated. Because the individual differences are removed, the D scores are usually much less variable than the original scores. Again, a smaller variance will produce a smaller standard error, which will increase the likelihood of a significant t statistic.

Finally, you should realize that there are potential disadvantages to using a repeated-measures design instead of independent-measures. Because the repeated-measures design requires that each individual participate in more than one treatment, there is always the risk that exposure to the first treatment will cause a change in the participants that influences their scores in the second treatment. For example, practice in the first treatment may cause improved performance in the second treatment. Thus, the scores in the second treatment may show a difference, but the difference is not caused by the second treatment. When participation in one treatment influences the scores in another treatment, the results may be distorted by **order effects**, and this can be a serious problem in repeated-measures designs.

LEARNING OBJECTIVES

1. Know the difference between independent-measures and repeated-measures research designs.

2. Know the difference between a repeated-measures and a matched-subjects research design.

3. Be able to perform the computations for the repeated-measures t test.

4. Be able to compute measures of effect size for the repeated-measures t.

5. Understand the advantages and disadvantages of the repeated-measures design (compared to an independent-measures design) and when this type of study is appropriate.

NEW TERMS AND CONCEPTS

The following terms were introduced in this chapter. You should be able to define or describe each term and, where appropriate, describe how each term is related to other terms in the list.

repeated-measures design	A research study where the same sample of individuals is measured in all of the treatment conditions.
matched-samples design	A research study where the individuals in one sample are matched one-to-one with the individuals in a second sample. The matching is based on a variable considered relevant to the study.
related-samples t statistic	The single sample t statistic applied to a sample of difference scores (D values) and the corresponding population of difference scores.
difference scores	The difference between two measurements obtained for a single subject. $D = X_2 - X_1$
estimated standard error of M_D	An estimate of the standard distance between a sample mean difference M_D and the population mean difference μ_D
individual differences	The naturally occurring differences from one individual to another that may cause the individuals to have different scores. The effects of participating in one treatment that may

order effects   influence the scores in the following treatment.

NEW FORMULAS

$$D = X_2 - X_1 \qquad\qquad M_D = \frac{\Sigma D}{N}$$

$$t = \frac{M_D - \mu_D}{s_{M_D}}$$

$$s_{M_D} = \sqrt{\frac{s^2}{n}} \qquad \text{or} \qquad s_{M_D} = \frac{s}{\sqrt{n}}$$

$$\text{estimated Cohen's d} = \frac{M_D}{s}$$

STEP BY STEP

Hypothesis Testing with the Related-Samples t. The related-samples t statistic is used to test for a mean difference (μ_D) between two treatment conditions, using data from a single sample of subjects where each individual is measured first in one treatment condition and then in the second condition. This test statistic also is used for matched-subjects designs, which consists of two samples with the subjects in one sample matched one-to-one with the subjects in the second sample. Often, a repeated-measures experiment consists of a "before/after" design where each subject is measured before treatment and then again after treatment. The following example will be used to demonstrate the related-samples t test.

A researcher would like to determine whether a particular treatment has an effect on performance scores. A sample of n = 16 subjects is selected. Each subject is measured before receiving the treatment and again after treatment. The researcher records the difference between the two scores for each subject. The difference scores averaged $M_D = -6$ with SS = 960.

Step 1: State the hypotheses and select an alpha level. In the experiment the treatment was given to a sample, but the researcher wants to determine whether the treatment has any effect for the general population. As always, the null hypothesis says that there is no effect.

H_0: $\mu_D = 0$ (on average, the before/after difference for the population is zero)
The alternative hypothesis states that the treatment does produce a difference.

H_1: $\mu_D \neq 0$

We will use $\alpha = .05$.

Step 2: Locate the critical region. With a sample of n = 16, the related-samples t statistic will have df = 15. Sketch the distribution of t statistics with df = 15 and locate the extreme 5% of the distribution. The critical boundaries are t = ±2.131.

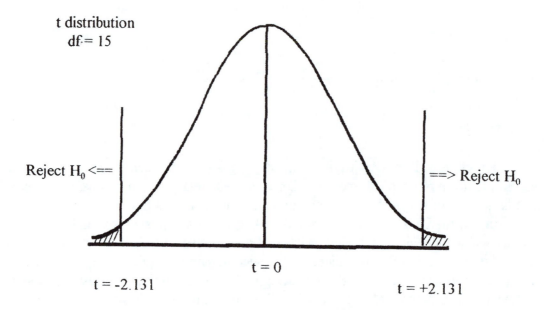

t distribution
df = 15

Reject H_0 <==

==> Reject H_0

t = 0

t = -2.131

t = +2.131

Step 3: Calculate the test statistic. As with all t statistics, it is easier to begin the calculation with the denominator of the t formula. For this example, the variance for the difference scores is

$$s^2 = \frac{SS}{n-1} = \frac{960}{15} = 64$$

With a sample of $n = 16$, the standard error is

$$s_{MD} = \sqrt{\frac{s^2}{n}} = \sqrt{\frac{64}{16}} = \frac{8}{4} = 2$$

Finally, substitute the sample mean difference and the standard error in the t formula,

$$t = \frac{M_D - \mu_D}{s_{MD}} = \frac{-6 - 0}{2} = \frac{-6}{2} = -3.00$$

Step 4: Make Decision. The t statistic is in the critical region. This is a very unlikely value for t if H_0 is true. Therefore, we reject H_0. The researcher concludes that the treatment does have a significant effect on performance scores.

Measuring Effect Size for the Repeated-Measures t
    We will use the data from the preceding example to demonstrate the calculation of Cohen's d and r^2. (Note that the sign of the mean difference is usually not included in the calculation of Cohen's d.)

$$\text{estimated Cohen's d} = \frac{M_D}{s} = \frac{6}{\sqrt{64}} = \frac{6}{8} = 0.75$$

$$r^2 = \frac{t^2}{t^2 + df} = \frac{(-3.00)^2}{(-3.00)^2 + 15} = \frac{9}{24} = 0.375$$

HINTS AND CAUTIONS

1. It is important to remember that the related-samples analysis is based on difference scores (D scores). Therefore, the computations of s^2 and s_{MD} are based on the sample of D scores.

2. When calculating the difference scores, be sure all of them are obtained by subtracting in the same direction. That is, you may either subtract 1st − 2nd, or 2nd − 1st as long as the same method is used throughout.

SELF TEST

True/False Questions

1. A researcher is evaluating the effectiveness of a new cholesterol medication by measuring cholesterol levels for a group of men before they take the medication and then measuring again after the men have been taking the medication for 4 months. This is an example of a repeated-measures study.

2. With a repeated-measures design, it is possible to evaluate the difference between two treatments using only one sample of subjects.

3. A researcher would like to compare two treatment conditions using a sample of 30 scores in each treatment. If a repeated-measures design is used, the study will require a total of $n = 60$ participants.

4. A repeated-measures t statistic with $df = 20$ indicates that a total of 21 subjects participated in the research study.

5. If a treatment has a consistent effect, then the sample of difference scores will have a large value for variance.

6. The null hypothesis for a repeated-measures t test concerns the entire population of difference scores, not just the D values in the sample.

7. As the variance of the difference scores increases, the value of the t statistic also increases (farther from zero).

8. If all other factors are held constant, an increase in the magnitude of M_D will cause a decrease in the size of the t statistic.

9. In general, using a repeated-measures design to evaluate the difference between two treatments will produce a larger standard error than would be obtained using an independent-measures design to compare the same two treatments.

10. One concern with a repeated-measures design is that a participant's performance in one treatment condition may be influenced by previous experience in another treatment condition.

Multiple Choice Questions

1. A repeated-measures study would *not* be appropriate for which of the following situations?
    a. A researcher would like to study the effect of practice on performance.
    b. A researcher would like to compare individuals from two different populations.
    c. The effect of a treatment is studied in a small group of individuals with a rare disease.
    d. A developmental psychologist examines how behavior unfolds by observing the same group of children at different ages.

2. For a repeated-measures hypothesis test, the null hypothesis states :
    a. For the individuals in the entire population there is no consistent difference between the two treatments.
    b. For the individuals in the entire population there is a consistent difference between the two treatments.
    c. For the individuals in the sample there is no consistent difference between the two treatments.
    d. For the individuals in the sample there is a consistent difference between the two treatments.

3. What is the value of M_D for the following set of difference scores?
    Scores: 3, –8, 6, –4, –2
    a. –1
    b. –5
    c. 23
    d. 23/5 = 4.6

4. A repeated-measures experiment with a sample of n = 16 subjects would produce a t statistic with df = ____ .
    a. 15
    b. 16
    c. 30
    d. 32

5. The following data were obtained from a repeated-measures research study. What is the value of df for the t statistic?

			Subject	1st	2nd
a.	df = 4		#1	8	10
b.	df = 5		#2	6	12
c.	df = 8		#3	10	7
d.	df = 9		#4	9	17
			#5	7	14

6. What is the value for the estimated standard error for a set of n = 9 D-scores with SS = 72?
   a. 72
   b. 9
   c. 3
   d. 1

7. A repeated-measures experiment and an independent-measures experiment both produce t statistics with df = 20. Which experiment used more participants?
   a. repeated measures
   b. independent measures
   c. They both used n = 21 subjects.
   d. They both used n = 22 subjects.

8. In general, what characteristics of the data (difference scores) are most likely to produce a significant t statistic for the repeated-measures hypothesis test?
   a. a large mean difference and large variance
   b. a large mean difference and small variance
   c. a small mean difference and large variance
   d. a small mean difference and small variance

9. A group of participants is measured before and after a treatment in a repeated-measures study. If the treatment has a consistent effect on all of the participants, then the difference scores should show _____.
   a. a large mean difference
   b. a small mean difference
   c. a large variance
   d. a small variance

10. A researcher is using a repeated-measures study to evaluate the difference between two treatments. If there is a consistent difference between the treatments then the data should produce _____.
   a. a small variance for the difference scores and a small standard error
   b. a small variance for the difference scores and a large standard error
   c. a large variance for the difference scores and a small standard error
   d. a large variance for the difference scores and a large standard error

11. The data from a repeated-measures research study show that the difference between treatment I and treatment II is large and positive for some subjects, large and negative for some subjects, and near zero for some subjects. These data will produce
   a. a small sample variance and a large t statistic.
   b. a small sample variance and a small t statistic.
   c. a large sample variance and a large t statistic.
   d. a large sample variance and a small t statistic.

12. A research report describing the results from a repeated-measures study states, "The data showed a significant difference between treatments, $t(22) = 4.71$, $p < .01$." From this report you can conclude that _____.
   a. a total of 22 individuals participated in the study
   b. a total of 23 individuals participated in the study
   c. a total of 24 individuals participated in the study
   d. It is impossible to determine the number of participants from the information given.

13. For which of the following situations would a repeated-measures design have a substantial advantage over an independent-measures design.
   a. few subjects are available and individual differences are large
   b. few subjects are available and individual differences are small
   c. many subjects are available and individual differences are large
   d. many subjects are available and individual differences are small

14. A researcher conducts a repeated-measures study comparing two treatment conditions with a sample of $n = 10$ participants and obtains a t statistic of $t = 2.01$. Which of the following is the correct decision about the null hypothesis.
   a. Reject the null hypothesis with $\alpha = .05$ but fail to reject with $\alpha = .01$.
   b. Reject the null hypothesis with either $\alpha = .05$ or $\alpha = .01$.
   c. Fail to reject the null hypothesis with either $\alpha = .05$ or $\alpha = .01$.
   d. cannot determine the correct decision without more information

15. Which of the following would have little or no influence on effect size as measured by Cohen's d or by r^2?
   a. Increasing the sample size
   b. Increasing the sample mean difference
   c. Increasing the sample variance
   d. All of the other three options would influence the magnitude of effect size.

Other Questions

1. A researcher would like to conduct a study comparing two treatment conditions with 30 individuals measured in each treatment.
   a. How many participants would be needed if the researcher uses an independent-measures design?
   b. How many participants would be needed if the researcher uses a repeated-measures design?
   c. How many participants would be needed if the researcher uses a matched-subjects design?

2. The following data represent the results from a repeated-measures study comparing two treatment conditions.

	Treatment		
Participant	1st	2nd	D
#1	8	14	
#2	6	11	
#3	10	10	
#4	9	11	
#5	7	12	
#6	10	16	

   a. Calculate the difference scores and compute the mean difference, M_D, and the variance for the sample of difference scores.
   b. Do the results indicate a significant difference between the two treatments? Use a two-tailed test with $\alpha = .05$.
   c. Calculate r^2 and the estimated Cohen's d to measure the size of the treatment effect.

3. A researcher would like to test the effect of a new diet drug on the activity level of animals. A sample of $n = 16$ rats is obtained and each rat's activity level is measured on an exercise wheel for one hour prior to receiving the drug. Thirty minutes after receiving the drug, each rat is again tested on the activity wheel. The data show that the rats increased

their activity by an average of $M_D = 21$ revolutions with SS = 6000 after receiving the drug. Do these data indicate that the drug had a significant effect on activity. Test at the .05 level.

    a. Using symbols, state the hypotheses for this test.
    b. Locate the critical region for $\alpha = .05$.
    c. Compute the t statistic for these data.
    d. What decision should the researcher make?
    e. Compute the effect size for this study using r^2 (the percentage of variance accounted for).

ANSWERS TO SELF TEST

True/False Answers

1. True
2. True
3. False. The same 30 subjects will be used in both treatment conditions.
4. True
5. False. A consistent effect will produce small variance for the difference scores.
6. True
7. False. The larger the variance, the smaller the value for t.
8. False. The larger the mean difference, the larger the value for t.
9. False. The repeated-measures study has a smaller standard error because the variance is reduced by removing individual differences.
10. True

Multiple-Choice Answers

1. b Two different populations will require two different samples.
2. a The null hypothesis states that there is no difference for the entire population.
3. a The five difference scores sum to -5. The mean is -1.
4. a df = n - 1
5. a df = n - 1
6. d The variance is 9 and the standard error is the square root of 9/9.
7. b The independent-measures study requires 22 participants and the repeated-measures study requires only 21.

8. b The most convincing sample has the biggest mean difference and the smallest variance.

9. d A consistent effect will produce small variance for the difference scores.

10. a A consistent effect produces a small variance and a large t statistic.

11. d Widely scattered scores produce a large variance and a small t statistic.

12. b $df = 22 = n - 1$. $n = 23$

13. a The repeated-measures design requires few participants and removes the individual differences.

14. c With $df = 9$, the critical values are 2.262 and 3.250.

15. a Sample size has little or no influence on measures of effect size.

Other Answers

1. a. An independent-measures design would require two separate samples of $n = 30$ for a total of 60 subjects.
   b. A repeated-measures design would require only one sample of $n = 30$ subjects.
   c. A matched-subjects design would require two matched samples of $n = 30$ for a total of 60 subjects.

2. a.

	Treatment		
Participant	1st	2nd	D
#1	8	14	+6
#2	6	11	+5
#3	10	10	0
#4	9	11	+2
#5	7	12	+5
#6	10	16	+6

$\Sigma D = 24$

$M_D = 24/6 = 4$

$s^2 = 30/5 = 6$

   b. The estimated standard error is 1, and $t = 4/1 = 4.00$. With $df = 5$, the critical value is $t = \pm 2.571$. Reject the null hypothesis and conclude that there is a significant difference between the two treatments.
   c. estimated Cohen's $d = 4/\sqrt{6} = 1.63$ and $r = 16/(16 + 5) = 0.762$

3. a. $H_0: \mu_D = 0$ (no effect). $H_1: \mu_D \neq 0$.
   b. With $df = 15$ and $\alpha = .05$, the critical value are $t = \pm 2.131$.
   c. The sample variance is $s^2 = 400$, the standard error is 5 points, and $t(15) = 4.2$.
   d. Reject the null hypothesis. The diet drug has a significant effect on activity.
   e. For these data, $r^2 = 17.64/32.64 = 0.54$ (or 54%)

CHAPTER 12

ESTIMATION

CHAPTER SUMMARY

The goals of Chapter 12 are:
1. To introduce the statistical technique of estimation as an alternative to a hypothesis test.
2. To demonstrate point and interval estimates for the single-sample t, the independent-measures t, and the repeated-measures t.
3. To demonstrate how the width of a confidence interval is related to the sample size and the level of confidence.

Estimation

In general terms, **estimation** uses a sample statistic as the basis for estimating the value of the corresponding population parameter. Although estimation and hypothesis testing are similar in many respects, they are complementary inferential processes. A hypothesis test is used to determine whether or not a treatment has an effect, while estimation is used to determine how much effect.

This complementary nature is demonstrated when estimation is used after a hypothesis test that resulted in rejecting the null hypothesis. In this situation, the hypothesis test has established that a treatment effect exists and the next logical step is to determine how much effect. It is also common to use estimation in situations where a researcher simply wants to learn about an unknown population. In this case, a sample is selected from the population and the sample data are then used to estimate the population parameters.

You should keep in mind that even though estimation and hypothesis testing are inferential procedures, these two techniques differ in terms of the type of question they address. A hypothesis test, for example, addresses the somewhat academic question concerning the *existence* of a treatment effect. Estimation, on the other hand, is directed toward the more practical question of *how much* effect.

The estimation process can produce either a **point estimate** or an **interval estimate**. A point estimate is a single value and has the advantage of being very precise. For example, based on sample data, you might estimate that the mean age for students at the state college is $\mu = 21.5$ years. An interval estimate consists of a range of values and has the advantage of providing greater confidence than a point estimate. For example, you might estimate that the mean age for students is somewhere between 20 and 23 years. Note that the interval estimate is less precise, but gives more confidence. For this reason, interval estimates are usually called **confidence intervals**.

Estimation with the Three t Statistics

There is an estimation procedure that accompanies each of the three t tests presented in the preceding three chapters. The estimation process begins with the same t statistic that is used for the corresponding hypothesis test. These all have the same conceptual structure:

$$t = \frac{\text{sample statistic - unknown parameter}}{\text{standard error}}$$

The basic estimation equation is obtained by solving this equation for the unknown parameter:

unknown parameter = statistic $\pm$ (t)(standard error)

For the single sample t, the unknown parameter is the population mean, μ. For the independent-measures t, the parameter is the difference between population means, $\mu_1 - \mu_2$, and for the repeated-measures t, the unknown parameter is the population mean difference, μ_D. To use the estimation equation, you first must obtain a value for t by estimating the location of the data within the appropriate t distribution. For a point estimate, a value of zero is used for t, yielding a single value for your estimate of the unknown population parameter. For interval estimates, you first select a level of confidence and then find the corresponding interval range of t values in the t distribution table. The estimated value for t (or range of values) is then substituted in the equation along with the values for the sample statistic and the standard error. The equation is then solved for the unknown parameter.

Factors Influencing the Width of a Confidence Interval

If other factors are held constant, increasing the level of confidence (for example, from 80% to 90%), will cause in increase in the width of the confidence interval. To obtain greater confidence, you must use a wider range of t statistic values, which results in a wider interval. On the other hand, increasing the sample size will cause a decrease in the width of the confidence interval. In simple terms, a larger sample gives you more information, which means that you can estimate the population parameter with more precision.

LEARNING OBJECTIVES

1. You should be able to use sample data to make a point estimate or an interval estimate of an unknown population mean using a single sample t statistic.

2. You should be able to make a point estimate or an interval estimate of a population mean difference using sample data from an independent-measures or a repeated-measures study.

3. You should understand how the size of a sample influences the width of a confidence interval.

4. You should understand how the level of confidence (the % confidence) influences the width of a confidence interval.

NEW TERMS AND CONCEPTS

The following terms were introduced in this chapter. You should be able to define or describe each term and, where appropriate, describe how each term is related to other terms in the list.

estimation   The inferential process of using a sample statistic to
                                estimate the value of an unknown population
                                parameter.

point estimate   A single number is used to estimate the value of an
                                unknown parameter. The result is a precise estimate,
                                but without confidence.

interval estimate   A range of values is used to estimate an unknown
                                parameter. The result is a less precise estimate but
                                there is a gain in confidence.

confidence interval	An interval estimate that is described in terms of the level (percentage) of confidence in the accuracy of the estimation.

NEW FORMULAS

$$\mu = M \pm ts_M$$

$$\mu_D = M_D \pm ts_{M_D}$$

$$(\mu_1 - \mu_2) = (M_1 - M_2) \pm ts_{M_1 - M_2}$$

STEP BY STEP

Estimation with the t statistic: The following example will be used to demonstrate the step-by-step procedures for estimation with the t statistic.

A researcher begins with a normal population with $\mu = 60$. The researcher is evaluating a specific treatment that is expected to increase scores. The treatment is administered to a sample of $n = 16$ individuals, and the mean for the treated sample is $M = 66$ with $SS = 1215$. The goal is to estimate the size of the treatment effect.

Step 1: Begin with the basic formula for estimation. Again, this is simply the regular t formula that has been solved for μ. For the single-sample t statistic,

$$\mu = M \pm ts_M$$

Step 2: Determine whether you are computing a point estimate or an interval estimate. If you want an interval, you must specify a level of confidence. We will compute a point estimate and a 90% confidence interval for the unknown population mean.

Step 3: Find the appropriate t values to substitute in the equation. For a point estimate, always use $t = 0$ which is the point in the exact middle of the distribution.

For a 90% confidence interval, we want the t values that form the boundaries for the middle 90% of the distribution. These values are obtained from the t distribution table using df = n - 1 = 15. You should find that 90% of the t statistics with df = 15 are located between t = +1.753 and t = −1.753.

Step 4: Compute M and s_M from the sample data. For this example we are given M = 66 and you can compute

$$s^2 = \frac{SS}{n-1} = \frac{1215}{15} = 81$$

$$s_M = \sqrt{\frac{s^2}{n}} = \sqrt{\frac{81}{16}} = \frac{9}{4} = 2.25$$

Step 5: Substitute the appropriate values in the estimation equation.

point estimate	interval estimate
$\mu = 66 \pm 0$	$\mu = 66 \pm (1.753)(2.25)$
$\mu = 66$	$\mu = 66 \pm 3.94$
Estimate $\mu = 66$	Estimate μ between 62.06 and 69.94

HINTS AND CAUTIONS

1. When computing a confidence interval after a hypothesis test, many students incorrectly take the t value that was computed in the hypothesis test and use this value in the estimation equation. Remember, the t value in the estimation equation is determined by the level of confidence and is obtained from the t distribution table.

2. When trying to locate the appropriate t value for a confidence interval, remember to use the "proportion in two tails" column of the t table. For an 80% confidence interval, for example, there would be 20% of the distribution left in the two tails and you should use the .20 column for two tails of the distribution.

SELF TEST

True/False Questions

1. For confidence intervals, precision increases as the interval gets wider.

2. Estimation is used to determine whether or not a treatment effect has occurred.

3. The sample mean (or mean difference) is always used as the point estimate of the population mean (or mean difference).

4. Increasing the level of confidence from 80% to 95% will increase the width of a confidence interval. (Assume all other factors are held constant.)

5. Increasing the number of scores in a sample from $n = 10$ to $n = 20$ will increase the width of a confidence interval to estimate the population mean. (Assume all other factors are held constant.)

6. A sample in treatment I has a mean of $M = 12$ with $SS = 23$. A second sample is given treatment II and has $M = 16$ with $SS = 29$. If these data are used to estimate the population mean difference between the two treatments, then the point estimate would be 4 points.

7. Estimation is often used after a hypothesis test for which the decision is "fail to reject the null hypothesis."

8. If an 80% confidence interval and a 90% confidence interval are constructed from the same sample data, then the 80% interval will be contained within the 90% interval.

9. An educational psychologist gives a group of third-grade students a reading test at the beginning of the school year and again at the end of the year. The psychologist wants to use the data to estimate how much reading scores change during the year. The psychologist should use the independent-measures t statistic for the estimation.

10. A sample of $n = 25$ scores is being used to construct an 80% confidence interval for the population mean. The correct t values for the estimation equation are ± 1.318.

1. In general, the goal of estimation is to _____.
    a. determine whether or not a treatment has any effect
    b. determine whether the effect of a treatment is to increase or to decrease scores
    c. determine how much effect a treatment has
    d. determine whether the sample accurately represents the population

2. Compared to an interval estimate, a point estimate _____.
    a. has greater precision and greater confidence
    b. has greater precision but less confidence
    c. has less precision but greater confidence
    d. has less precision and less confidence

3. A single sample with $n = 25$ scores is used to construct a confidence interval for the population mean. What would be the difference between a 90% confidence interval and a 95% confidence interval?
    a. The 90% interval will be wider and will have larger values for t.
    b. The 90% interval will be wider and will have smaller values for t.
    c. The 90% interval will be narrower and will have larger values for t.
    d. The 90% interval will be narrower and will have smaller values for t.

4. A researcher obtains a sample of $n = 25$ individuals from a population with unknown parameters. The goal is to use the sample to estimate the population mean. If the sample mean is $M = 84$ and $SS = 2400$, then what value should be used as the point estimate of μ?
    a. 0
    b. 25
    c. 84
    d. cannot answer without additional information

5. A researcher uses a sample of $n = 25$ scores to construct a 90% confidence interval to estimate an unknown population mean. The correct interpretation of the confidence interval is:
    a. If another sample of $n = 25$ scores was selected, there is a 90% probability that the sample mean will be in the interval.
    b. There is a 90% probability that this particular interval contains the population mean.
    c. All of the above.
    d. None of the above.

6. Which combination of factors would definitely *increase* the width of a confidence interval?
  a. use a larger sample and increase the level of confidence
  b. use a smaller sample and increase the level of confidence
  c. use a larger sample and decrease the level of confidence
  d. use a smaller sample and decrease the level of confidence

7. A researcher obtains a sample of $n = 25$ individuals from a population with unknown parameters. If the sample mean is $M = 84$ and $SS = 2400$, then what value(s) of t should be used to construct a 90% confidence interval to estimate the population mean?
  a. ± 1.316
  b. ± 1.318
  c. ± 1.708
  d. ± 1.711

8. A researcher obtains a sample of $n = 25$ individuals from a population with unknown parameters. The goal is to use the sample to estimate the population mean. If the sample mean is $M = 84$ and $SS = 2400$, then the 80% confidence interval would be _____.
  a. $\mu = 84 \pm 10(1.318)$
  b. $\mu = 84 \pm 2(1.318)$
  c. $\mu = 84 \pm 10(1.711)$
  d. $\mu = 84 \pm 2(1.711)$

9. A researcher would like to determine the average mathematical skill level for freshmen entering the college. A sample of $n = 30$ freshmen is obtained and each person is given a standardized mathematics skills test. The researcher plans to use the sample data to estimate the mean score for the entire population of freshmen. Which estimation equation should the researcher use?
  a. the single-sample t equation
  b. the independent-measures t equation
  c. the repeated-measures t equation
  d. cannot determine without additional information

10. What value(s) can be estimated using the repeated-measures t statistic?
  a. the value of an unknown population mean
  b. the difference between two population means
  c. the mean for the entire population of difference scores
  d. the values for two different population means

11. A researcher knows that a special reading program will improve students' reading scores. To determine how much improvement will occur, the researcher obtains a sample of $n = 25$ students and measures each individual's reading performance before and after the special program. The data will be used to estimate the mean amount of improvement. Which estimation equation should the researcher use?
    a. the single-sample t equation
    b. the independent-measures t equation
    c. the repeated-measures t equation
    d. cannot determine without additional information

12. A sample of $n = 16$ college students is used to evaluate the effectiveness of a new Study Skills Workshop. Each student's grade point average (GPA) is recorded for the semester before the workshop and for the semester after the workshop. The average GPA improved by $M_D = 0.60$ points with $s^2 = 0.16$. The researcher would like to use the sample to estimate how much effect the workshop would have for the entire college population. What values of t should be used to construct a 95% confidence interval estimate of the population mean difference?
    a. ± 2.120
    b. ± 2.131
    c. ± 1.746
    d. ± 1.753

13. A researcher would like to determine how much difference there is between two treatment conditions. A sample of $n = 10$ people is tested in the first treatment and produces a mean score of $M = 48$ with $SS = 200$. A second sample of $n = 10$ people is tested in the second treatment and produces $M = 42$ with $SS = 160$. If the researcher used these data to make a point estimate of the population mean difference, then what would the estimate be?
    a. $\mu_1 - \mu_2 = 6$
    b. $\mu_1 - \mu_2 = 40$
    c. $\mu_1 - \mu_2 = 42$
    d. $\mu_1 - \mu_2 = 48$

14. The 90% confidence interval for the difference between two population means extends from 4.00 to 8.00. Based on this information you can conclude that the difference between the two sample means was _____.
    a. 2 points
    b. 4 points
    c. 6 points
    d. 8 points

15. A sample of $n = 16$ college students is used to evaluate the effectiveness of a new Study Skills Workshop. Each student's grade point average (GPA) is recorded for the semester before the workshop and for the semester after the workshop. The average GPA improved by $M_D = 0.60$ points with $s^2 = 0.16$. The researcher would like to use the sample to estimate how much effect the workshop would have for the entire college population. What value should be used as the point estimate of the population mean difference?

    a. 0
    b. 0.60
    c. 0.16
    d. 16

Other Questions

1. Estimation often is used after a hypothesis test. Although these two inferential techniques involve many of the same calculations, they are intended to answer different questions.

    a. In general terms, what information is provided by a hypothesis test and what information is provided by estimation?
    b. Explain why it would not be appropriate to use estimation after a hypothesis test where the decision was "fail to reject" the null hypothesis.

2. A researcher would like to evaluate the reading ability of fourth-grade students in the city school district. A sample of $n = 36$ students is obtained and the students are given a standardized reading test for which the nationwide fourth-grade average is $\mu = 40$. The students in the sample averaged $M = 42.5$ with $SS = 2835$.

    a. Make a point estimate of the mean reading score for the entire population of city school fourth-grade students. How do they compare with the national average?
    b. Make an interval estimate of the population mean so that you are 90% confident that the new mean is in your interval. Again, how do the city school students compare with the national average?

3. A researcher would like to evaluate the effect of a regular exercise program on the health and well being of elderly adults. A sample of 16 participants is obtained from a local senior center and each person completes a life-satisfaction questionnaire. Then the participants are enrolled in an exercise class that meets twice weekly for one hour. After six weeks, each participant again completes the life-satisfaction questionnaire. On average, the participants scored $M_D = 8$ points higher after the program with $SS = 960$.

a. On the basis of these data, can the counselor conclude that the exercise program has a significant effect on well being? Test at the .05 level of significance.
b. Use the data to make a point estimate of how much improvement results from regular exercise.
c. Make an interval estimate of the mean improvement so that you are 90% confident that the true mean is contained in your interval.

4. The government has developed a pamphlet listing driving tips that are designed to promote fuel economy. To test the effectiveness of these tips, a sample of twenty families is obtained, all with identical cars and similar driving habits. Ten of these families are given the pamphlet and instructions to follow the driving tips carefully. The other ten families are simply instructed to monitor their gas mileage for a two-week period. At the end of two weeks, the gas mileage figures for both groups are as follows:

Experimental Group with Pamphlet	Control Group no Pamphlet
n = 10	n = 10
M = 25.7	M = 21.6
SS = 160	SS = 128

a. Do these data indicate that the driving tips have a significant effect on gas mileage? Test at the .05 level of significance.
b. Use the data to make a point estimate of how much improvement in gas mileage results from following the tips.
c. Use the data to construct a 90% confidence interval to estimate how much effect the driving tips have on gas mileage.

ANSWERS TO SELF TEST

True/False Answers

1. False. A wider interval indicates lower precision.
2. False. A hypothesis test is used to determine whether or not a treatment has an effect. Estimation is used to determine how much effect.
3. True
4. True
5. False. A larger sample provides a more precise estimate (narrower interval)
6. True

7. False. Failing to reject the null hypothesis means that you have concluded that the treatment has no effect. In this case, it would make no sense to estimate "how much" effect.
8. True
9. False. This is a repeated-measures study.
10. True

Multiple-Choice Answers

1. c The goal of estimation is to determine *how much* effect.
2. b A point estimate gives precision and an interval estimate gives confidence.
3. d The greater the confidence, the larger the t values and the wider the interval.
4. c Always use the sample mean as the point estimate of μ.
5. b The interval is constructed so that there is a 90% probability that it contains the population mean.
6. b High confidence and a small sample combine to produce a wide interval.
7. d With df = 24 and 0.10 in two tails combined, t = ±1.711.
8. b The sample has df = 24 and an estimated standard error of 2 points.
9. a To estimate one population mean requires only one sample mean.
10. c The repeated-measures t uses a sample of difference scores to estimate μ_D.
11. c The same students are measured twice. This is a repeated-measures study.
12. b For df = 15 and 95% confidence, use t = ±2.131.
13. a The sample mean difference is used as the point estimate.
14. c The sample mean (or mean difference) is always in the center of the confidence interval.
15. b The sample mean difference is used as the point estimate.

Other Answers

1. a. A hypothesis test is intended to determine whether or not a treatment effect exists. Estimation is used to determine how much effect.
   b. If the decision from the hypothesis test is "fail to reject H_0"then the data do not provide sufficient evidence to conclude that there is any treatment effect. In this case, it would not be reasonable to use estimation in an attempt to determine "how much" effect exists.

2. a. Use the sample mean, $M = 42.5$ as the point estimate of μ. The students appear to be slightly above the national average.

   b. The 90% confidence interval would be $\mu = 42.5 \pm (1.697)(1.5)$. The interval extends from 39.95 to 45.05. Again, the students appear to be somewhat above average, however there may be no difference at all because the national mean is contained within the interval.

3. a. With $s^2 = 64$ and $s_{MD} = 2$, the data have a t statistic of $t = 4.00$. Reject H_0 and conclude that the exercise has a significant effect.

   b. Use the sample mean, $M_D = 8$ points, as the point estimate of μ_D.

   c. The 90% confidence interval would be $\mu_D = 8 \pm (1.753)(2)$, which gives a mean improvement between 4.494 to 11.506.

4. a. The pooled variance is 16 and the estimated standard error is 1.79. The t statistic is $t = 2.29$. Reject H_0.

   b. The sample mean difference, 4.1 miles per gallon, is the best point estimate.

   c. The 90% confidence interval would be $\mu_1 - \mu_2 = 4.1 \pm (1.734)(1.79)$, which gives an interval estimate between 1.00 and 7.2 miles per gallon.

CHAPTER 13

INTRODUCTION TO ANALYSIS OF VARIANCE

CHAPTER SUMMARY

The goals of Chapter 13 are:

1. To introduce the logical foundation for analysis of variance.
2. To demonstrate the process of hypothesis testing with analysis of variance.
3. To demonstrate the use of post tests to help interpret the results from an analysis of variance.
4. To demonstrate the measurement of effect size for an analysis of variance.
5. To demonstrate the relationship between analysis of variance and the independent-measures t test for a study comparing exactly two samples or treatment conditions.

The Logic and the Process of Analysis of Variance

Chapter 13 presents the general logic and basic formulas for the hypothesis testing procedure known as **analysis of variance** (ANOVA). The purpose of ANOVA is much the same as the t tests presented in the preceding three chapters: the goal is to determine whether the mean differences that are obtained for sample data are sufficiently large to justify a conclusion that there are mean differences between the populations from which the samples were obtained. The difference between ANOVA and the t tests is that ANOVA can be used in situations where there are *two or more* means being compared, whereas the t tests are limited to situations where only two means are involved.

Analysis of variance is necessary to protect researchers from excessive risk of a Type I error in situations where a study is comparing more than two population means. These situations would require a series of several t tests to evaluate all of the mean differences. (Remember, a t test can compare only 2 means at a time.) Although each t test can be done with a specific α-level (risk of Type I error), the α-levels accumulate over a series of tests so that the final **experimentwise α-level** can be quite large. ANOVA allows researcher to evaluate all of the mean differences in a single hypothesis test using a single α-level and, thereby, keeps the risk of a Type I error under control no matter how many different means are being compared.

Although ANOVA can be used in a variety of different research situations, this chapter presents only independent-measures designs involving only one independent variable.

The test statistic for ANOVA is an F-ratio, which is a ratio of two sample variances. In the context of ANOVA, the sample variances are called **mean squares**, or **MS** values. The top of the F-ratio $MS_{between}$ measures the size of mean differences between samples. The bottom of the ratio MS_{within} measures the magnitude of differences that would be expected without any treatment effects.

Thus, the F-ratio has the same basic structure as the independent-measures t statistic presented in Chapter 10.

$$F = \frac{\text{obtained mean differences (including treatment effects)}}{\text{differences expected by chance (without treatment effects)}} = \frac{MS_{between}}{MS_{within}}$$

A large value for the F-ratio indicates that the obtained sample mean differences are greater than would be expected if the treatments had no effect.

Each of the sample variances, MS values, in the F-ratio is computed using the basic formula for sample variance:

$$\text{sample variance} = MS = \frac{SS}{df}$$

To obtain the SS and df values, you must go through an analysis that separates the total variability for the entire set of data into two basic components: between-treatment variability (which will become the numerator of the F-ratio), and within-treatment variability (which will be the denominator). The two components of the F-ratio can be described as follows:

Between-Treatments Variability: $MS_{between}$ measures the size of the differences between the sample means. For example, suppose that three treatments, each with a sample of n = 5 subjects, have means of $M_1 = 1$, $M_2 = 2$, and $M_3 = 3$. Notice that the three means are different; that is, they are variable. By computing the variance for the three means we can measure the size of the differences. Although it is possible to compute a variance for the set of sample means, it usually is easier to use the total, T, for each sample instead of the mean, and compute variance for the set of T values. Logically, the differences (or variance) between means can be caused by two sources:

1. Treatment Effects: If the treatments have different effects, this could cause the mean for one treatment to be higher (or lower) than the mean for another treatment.
2. Chance or Sampling Error: If there is no treatment effect at all, you would still expect some differences between samples. Mean differences from one sample to another are an example of *sampling error*, a concept that was first introduced in Figure 1.2 in your textbook.

Within-Treatments Variability: MS_{within} measures the size of the differences that exist *inside* each of the samples. Because all the individuals in a sample receive exactly the same treatment, any differences (or variance) within a sample cannot be caused by different treatments. Thus, these differences are caused by only one source:
1. Chance or Error: The unpredictable differences that exist between individual scores are not caused by any systematic factors and are simply considered to be due to chance or error.

Considering these sources of variability, the structure of the F-ratio becomes,

$$F = \frac{\text{treatment effect} + \text{chance/error}}{\text{chance/error}}$$

When the null hypothesis is true and there are no differences between treatments, the F-ratio is balanced. That is, when the "treatment effect" is zero, the top and bottom of the F-ratio are measuring the same variance. In this case, you should expect an F-ratio near 1.00. When the sample data produce an F-ratio near 1.00, we will conclude that there is no significant treatment effect.

On the other hand, a large treatment effect will produce a large value for the F-ratio. Thus, when the sample data produce a large F-ratio we will reject the null hypothesis and conclude that there are significant differences between treatments.

To determine whether an F-ratio is large enough to be significant, you must select an α-level, find the df values for the numerator and denominator of the F-ratio, and consult the F-distribution table to find the critical value.

Analysis of Variance and Post Tests

The null hypothesis for ANOVA states that for the general population there are no mean differences among the treatments being compared; H_0: $\mu_1 = \mu_2 = \mu_3 = \ldots$ When the null hypothesis is rejected, the conclusion is that there are significant mean differences. However, the ANOVA simply establishes that differences exist, it does not indicate exactly which treatments are different. With more than two treatments, this creates a problem. Specifically, you must follow the ANOVA with additional tests, called **post tests**, to determine exactly which treatments are different and which are not. The **Scheffe test** and **Tukey's HSD** are examples of post tests. These tests are done after an ANOVA where H_0 is rejected with more than two treatment conditions. The tests compare the treatments, two at a time, to test the significance of the mean differences.

Measuring Effect Size for an Analysis of Variance

As with other hypothesis tests, an ANOVA evaluates the *significance* of the sample mean differences; that is, are the differences bigger than would be reasonable to expect just by chance. With large samples, however, it is possible for relatively small mean differences to be statistically significant. Thus, the hypothesis test does not necessarily provide information about the actual size of the mean differences. To supplement the hypothesis test, it is recommended that you calculate a measure of effect size. For an analysis of variance the common technique for measuring effect size is to compute the percentage of variance that is accounted for by the treatment effects. For the t statistics, this percentage was identified as r^2, but in the context of ANOVA the percentage is identified as η^2 (the Greek letter eta, squared). The formula for computing effect size is:

$$\eta^2 = \frac{SS_{\text{between treatments}}}{SS_{\text{total}}}$$

LEARNING OBJECTIVES

1. You should be familiar with the purpose, terminology, and special notation of analysis of variance.

2. You should be able to perform an analysis of variance for the data from a single-factor, independent-measures experiment.

3. You should recognize when post hoc tests are necessary and you should be able to complete an analysis of variance using Tukey's HSD or the Scheffe post hoc test.

4. You should be able to report the results of an analysis of variance using either a summary table or an F-ratio (including df values). Also, you should be able to understand and interpret these reports when they appear in scientific literature.

5. You should be able to compute η^2 (the percentage of variance accounted for) as a measure of effect size for an analysis of variance.

NEW TERMS AND CONCEPTS

The following terms were introduced in this chapter. You should be able to define or describe each term and, where appropriate, describe how each term is related to other terms in the list.

factor	In analysis of variance, an independent variable (or quasi-independent variable) is called a factor.
levels of a factor	The specific conditions or values that are used to represent the factor are called levels.
F-ratio	The test statistic for analysis of variance is called an F-ratio and compares the differences (variance) between treatments with the differences (variance) that are expected by chance.
MS (Mean Square)	In analysis of variance, a sample variance is called a mean square or MS, indicating that variance measures the mean of the squared deviations.
post hoc test	A test that is conducted after an ANOVA with more than two treatment conditions where the null hypothesis was rejected. The purpose of post hoc tests is to determine exactly which treatment conditions are significantly different.
between-treatments SS, df, MS	Values used to measure and describe the differences between treatments (mean differences).
within-treatments SS, df, MS	Values used to measure and describe the differences inside the treatment conditions. These differences are assumed to measure chance or error variability.
total SS and df	Values used to measure and describe the total amount of variability for the entire set of data.
η^2 (eta squared)	A measure of effect size based on the percentage of variance accounted for by the sample mean differences.

NEW FORMULAS

$$SS_{total} = \Sigma X^2 - \frac{G^2}{N} \qquad df_{total} = N - 1$$

$$SS_{within} = \Sigma SS_{each\ treatment} \qquad df_{within} = \Sigma df_{each\ treatment} = N - k$$

$SS_{between}$ can be found by subtraction: $SS_{between} = SS_{total} - SS_{within}$
or computed:

$$SS_{between} = \Sigma \frac{T^2}{n} - \frac{G^2}{N} \quad or \quad n(SS_{means}) \qquad df_{between} = k - 1$$

$$MS = \frac{SS}{df} \qquad F = \frac{MS_{between}}{MS_{within}}$$

$$\eta^2 = \frac{SS_{between\ treatments}}{SS_{total}}$$

STEP BY STEP

Analysis of Variance: Analysis of variance is a hypothesis testing technique that is used to determine whether there are differences among the means of two or more populations. In this chapter we examined ANOVA for an independent-measures experiment, which means that the data consist of a separate sample for each treatment condition (or each population). Before you begin the actual analysis, you should complete all the preliminary calculations with the data, including T and SS for each sample, and G and ΣX^2 for the entire set of scores. The following example will be used to demonstrate ANOVA.

A researcher has obtained three different samples representing three populations. The data are as follows:

Sample 1	Sample 2	Sample 3	
0	6	6	
4	8	5	$G = 60$
0	5	9	
1	4	4	$\Sigma X^2 = 356$
0	2	6	
T = 5	T = 25	T = 30	
SS = 12	SS = 20	SS = 14	

Step 1: State the hypotheses and select an alpha level. The null hypothesis states that there are no mean differences among the three populations.

H_0: $\mu_1 = \mu_2 = \mu_3$

Remember, we generally do not try to list specific alternatives, but rather state a generic alternative hypothesis.

H_1: At least one population mean is different from another.

For this test we will use $\alpha = .05$.

Step 2: Locate the critical region. With k = 3 samples, the numerator of the F-ratio will have $df_{between}$ = k - 1 = 2. There are n = 5 scores in each sample. Within each sample there are n - 1 = 4 degrees of freedom, and summing across all three samples gives df_{within} = 4 + 4 + 4 = 12 for the denominator of the F-ratio. Thus, the F-ratio for this analysis will have df = 2, 12.

Sketch the entire distribution of F-ratios with df = 2, 12 and locate the extreme 5% of the distribution. The critical F value is 3.88.

F distribution
df = 2, 12

Fail to Reject H_0

Reject H_0

0

F = 3.88

Step 3: Compute the test statistic. It is best to work through the calculations in a systematic way. Compute all three parts of the analysis (total, between, and within) and check that the two components add to the total.

$$SS_{total} = \Sigma X^2 - \frac{G^2}{N} = 356 - \frac{(60)^2}{15}$$

$$= 356 - 240$$

$$= 116$$

$$SS_{within} = \Sigma SS = 12 + 20 + 14 = 46$$

SS_{bet} can be found by subtraction: $SS_{total} - SS_{within} = 116 - 46 = 70$ or, by calculation

$$SS_{bet} = \Sigma \frac{T^2}{n} - \frac{G^2}{N} = \frac{(5)^2}{5} + \frac{(25)^2}{5} + \frac{(30)^2}{5} - \frac{(60)^2}{15}$$

$$= 5 + 125 + 180 - 240$$

$$= 70$$

We have already found $df_{between}$ and df_{within}. To complete the analysis of df, compute
$$df_{total} = N - 1 = 15 - 1 = 14$$
(Check that $14 = 12 + 2$)

Next, compute the two variances (Mean Squares) that will form the F-ratio.

$$MS_{between} = \frac{SS_{between}}{df_{between}} = \frac{70}{2} = 35$$

$$MS_{within} = \frac{SS_{within}}{df_{within}} = \frac{46}{12} = 3.83$$

Finally, the F-ratio for these data is,

$$F = \frac{MS_{between}}{MS_{within}} = \frac{35}{3.83} = 9.14$$

Step 4: Make decision. The F-ratio for these data is in the critical region. The numerator is more than 9 times larger than the denominator which indicates a significant treatment effect. Reject H_0 and conclude that there are differences among the means of the three populations.

Measuring effect size with η^2

The data from the preceding example will be used to demonstrate the calculation of η^2 to measure effect size. For these data, $SS_{between\ treatments} = 70$ and $SS_{total} = 116$, so the percentage of variance accounted for by the treatment effects is

$$\eta^2 = \frac{SS_{between\ treatments}}{SS_{total}} = \frac{70}{116} = 0.603 \quad (60.3\%)$$

HINTS AND CAUTIONS

1. It may help you to understand analysis of variance if you remember that measuring variance is conceptually the same as measuring differences. The goal of the analysis is to determine whether the mean differences in the data are larger than would be expected if there was no treatment effect.

2. The formulas for SS between treatments and SS within treatments, and their role in the F-ratio, may be easier to remember if you look at the similarities between the independent-measures t formula and the F-ratio formula.

   a. The numerator of the t statistic measures the difference between the two sample means, $(M_1 - M_2)$. The numerator of the F-ratio also looks at differences between treatments by computing the variability for the treatment totals.

   b. The standard error in the denominator of the t statistic is computed by first pooling the two sample variances. This calculation uses the SS values from each of the two separate samples. The denominator of the F-ratio also uses the SS values from each of the separate samples to compute SS within treatments. In fact, when there are only two treatment conditions, the pooled variance from the t statistic is equivalent to the MS within treatments from the F-ratio.

SELF TEST

True/False Questions

1. The main advantage of analysis of variance, compared to t tests, is that ANOVA can be used to evaluate differences between variances as well as differences between means.

2. When the null hypothesis is true, the F-ratio for analysis of variance is expected, on average, to be zero.

3. In general, a large value for an F-ratio indicates that the null hypothesis is wrong.

4. The larger the differences between treatment means, the larger the F-ratio.

5. In an analysis of variance, if all other factors are held constant, the larger the sample variances, the bigger the value for the F-ratio.

6. For an analysis of variance comparing two treatments with $n = 5$ in each treatment, the F-ratio will have $df = 2, 8$.

7. The critical region for an analysis of variance is located entirely in one tail of the distribution.

8. An analysis of variance produces $SS_{between} = 30$ and $MS_{between} = 10$. The analysis is being used to compare the mean differences between 3 treatments.

9. Post tests are done after an analysis of variance to determine how much treatment effect there is.

10. Post tests are *not* necessary if the decision from the original ANOVA is to fail to reject the null hypothesis.

Multiple-Choice Questions

1. The distinction between the "testwise" alpha level and the "experimentwise" alpha level is important _____.
    a. whenever you do an analysis of variance
    b. when the study is comparing exactly two treatments
    c. when the study is comparing more than two treatments
    d. only when there are fewer than 30 scores in each treatment

2. In analysis of variance, the F-ratio is a ratio of _____.
    a. two (or more) sample means
    b. two variances
    c. sample means divided by sample variances
    d. None of the other 3 choices is correct.

3. An analysis of variance is used to evaluate the mean differences for a research study comparing four treatment conditions with a separate sample of $n = 5$ in each treatment. The analysis produces $SS_{within\ treatments} = 32$, $SS_{between\ treatments} = 40$, and $SS_{total} = 72$. For this analysis, what is $MS_{within\ treatments}$?
    a. 32/5
    b. 32/4
    c. 32/16
    d. 32/20

4. A researcher uses analysis of variance to test for mean differences among four treatments with a sample of $n = 6$ in each treatment. The F-ratio for this analysis would have what df values?
    a. df = 3, 5
    b. df = 3, 15
    c. df = 3, 20
    d. df = 4, 24

5. A researcher obtains an F-ratio with df = 1, 20 from an independent-measures research study comparing 2 treatment conditions. If the researcher had used an independent-measures t statistic to evaluate the data, what value would be obtained for degrees of freedom for the t statistic?
    a. df = 19
    b. df = 20
    c. df = 21
    d. cannot determine from the information given

6. In an analysis of variance, large mean differences from one sample to another will produce a large value for _____.
    a. $SS_{between\ treatments}$
    b. $SS_{within\ treatments}$
    c. SS_{total}
    d. Large mean differences will cause all three SS values to be large.

7. In analysis of variance, large values for the sample variances will produce a large value for_____.

    a. $SS_{between\ treatments}$
    b. $SS_{within\ treatments}$
    c. SS_{total}
    d. Large sample variances will cause all three SS values to be large.

8. In an ANOVA, which of the following is most likely to produce a large value for the F-ratio?

    a. large mean differences and small sample variances
    b. large mean differences and large sample variances
    c. small mean differences and small sample variances
    d. small mean differences and large sample variances

9. An analysis of variance is used to evaluate the mean differences among three treatment conditions. The analysis produces $SS_{within\ treatments} = 20$, $SS_{between\ treatments} = 40$, and $SS_{total} = 60$. For this analysis, what is $MS_{between\ treatments}$?

    a. 20/3
    b. 20/2
    c. 40/3
    d. 40/2

10. A research study compares three treatments with n = 5 in each treatment. If the SS values for the three treatments are 25, 20, and 15, then the analysis of variance would produce SS_{within} equal to _____.

    a. 12
    b. 20
    c. 60
    d. cannot be determined from the information given

11. An independent-measures t test produced a t statistic with df = 20. If the same data had been evaluated with an analysis of variance, what would be the df values for the F-ratio?

    a. 1, 19
    b. 1, 20
    c. 2, 19
    d. 2, 20

12. A research report concludes that there are significant differences among treatments, with "$F(2,27) = 8.62, p < .01$." How many treatment conditions were compared in this study?

    a. 2
    b. 3
    c. 29
    d. 30

13. Post hoc tests are necessary after an ANOVA whenever _____.

    a. H_0 is rejected
    b. there are more than two treatments
    c. H_0 is rejected and there are more than two treatments
    d. You *always* should do post hoc tests after an ANOVA.

14. A research study compares three treatments with $n = 5$ in each treatment. If the data were examined using an analysis of variance, the F-ratio would have df = _____.

    a. 12
    b. 14
    c. 2, 12
    d. 2, 14

15. An analysis of variance produces $SS_{between} = 40$ and $SS_{within} = 60$. Based on this information, the percentage of variance accounted for, η^2, is equal to _____.

    a. $40/60 = 67\%$
    b. $40/100 = 40\%$
    c. $60/40 = 150\%$
    d. $60/100 = 60\%$

Other Questions

1. The following data summarize the results of two experiments. Each experiment compares three treatment conditions, and each experiment uses separate samples of $n = 10$ for each treatment.

Experiment A				Experiment B		
Treatment				Treatment		
1	2	3		1	2	3
$M = 1$	$M = 3$	$M = 5$		$M = 1$	$M = 10$	$M = 20$
$s = 15$	$s = 12$	$s = 18$		$s = 3$	$s = 5$	$s = 4$

Just looking at the data - without doing any calculations - answer each of the following questions.

    a.   Which experiment will produce the larger $MS_{between}$?
    b.   Which experiment will produce the larger MS_{within}?
    c.   Which experiment will produce the larger F-ratio?

2. Use an analysis of variance with $\alpha = .05$ to determine whether the following data provide evidence of any significant differences among the three treatments.

Treatments

I	II	III	
0	4	1	$G = 30$
2	6	0	
2	1	3	$\Sigma X^2 = 114$
0	5	1	
1	4	0	
$T = 5$	$T = 20$	$T = 5$	
$SS = 4$	$SS = 14$	$SS = 6$	

3. A researcher conducts an experiment comparing three treatment conditions with a separate sample of $n = 8$ in each treatment. An analysis of variance is used to evaluate the data, and the results of the ANOVA are presented in the table below. Complete all missing values in the table.

Source	SS	df	MS	
Between Treatments	12	__	__	$F = 2.00$
Within Treatments	__	__	__	
Total	__	__		

ANSWERS TO SELF TEST
True/False Answers

1. False. Both tests evaluate mean differences.
2. False. When the null hypothesis is true, the F-ratio will have an average value of 1.00.
3. True
4. True
5. False. Larger sample variance produces a smaller F-ratio.

6. False.   The F-ratio would have df = 1, 8.
7. True
8. False.   MS = SS/df. In this case, there are 4 treatments.
9. False.   Post tests are done to determine exactly which treatments are
        significantly different.
10. True

Multiple-Choice Answers

1. c With more than two treatments, there will more than one mean difference
      to test.
2. b The F-ratio is MS between treatments divided by MS within.
3. c MS = SS/df and df within = 4 + 4 + 4 + 4 = 16
4. c df between = 3 and df within = 5 + 5 + 5 + 5 = 20.
5. b df within treatments and df for the t statistic are both $(n_1 - 1) + (n_2 - 1)$
6. a The between treatments SS measures the size of the mean differences.
7. b The within treatments SS adds the SS values from within the treatments.
8. a Mean differences contributed to the numerator and variance contributes to
      the denominator of the F-ratio.
9. d MS = SS/df and df between = 3 − 1 = 2.
10. c SS within = the sum of the SS values from within the treatments.
11. b df between = 2 − 1 = 1, and df within = $(n_1 - 1) + (n_2 - 1)$
12. b With df between = 2, there must be 3 treatments.
13. c Rejecting the null means that differences exist, and with k > 2 there is
       uncertainty as to where the differences are located.
14. c df between = 3 − 1, and df within = 4 + 4 + 4 = 12.
15. b The total SS = 40 + 60 = 100, and eta squared = 40/100.

Other Answers

1. a. Experiment B has larger mean differences which will produce a larger
       $MS_{between}$.
   b. Experiment A has larger sample standard deviations (more variance within
       samples) and will produce a larger MS_{within}.
   c. Experiment B has larger differences between treatments and smaller
       variability within treatments. This combination will produce a larger F-ratio.

2. The ANOVA is summarized as follows:

Source	SS	df	MS	
Between Treatments	30	2	15	$F = 7.50$
Within Treatments	24	12	2	
Total	54	14		

With $df = 2, 12$ the critical value is $F = 3.88$. Reject H_0 and conclude that there are significant differences among the three treatments.

3.

Source	SS	df	MS	
Between Treatments	12	2	6	$F = 2.00$
Within Treatments	63	21	3	
Total	75	23		

CHAPTER 14

REPEATED-MEASURES AND TWO-FACTOR
ANALYSIS OF VARIANCE

CHAPTER SUMMARY

The goals of Chapter 14 are:
1. To introduce the logic underlying the repeated-measures analysis of variance.
2. To demonstrate the similarities and differences between a repeated-measures ANOVA and an independent-measures ANOVA.
3. To introduce the concepts of main effects and interactions.
4. To demonstrate the process of hypothesis testing with the two-factor ANOVA.

The Logical Background for a Repeated-Measures ANOVA

Chapter 14 extends analysis of variance to research situations using repeated-measures or related-samples research designs. Much of the logic and many of the formulas for repeated-measures ANOVA are identical to the independent-measures analysis introduced in Chapter 13. However, the repeated-measures ANOVA includes a second stage of analysis in which variability due to **individual differences** is subtracted out of the error term. The repeated-measures design eliminates individual differences from the between-treatments variability (numerator of the F-ratio) because the same subjects are used in every treatment condition. To balance the F-ratio, however, the calculations require that individual differences also be eliminated from the denominator of the F-ratio. The result is a test statistic similar to the independent-measures F-ratio but with all individual differences removed.

Comparing Independent-Measures and Repeated-Measures ANOVA

Recall that the F-ratio for the independent-measures analysis of variance (Chapter 13) has the following structure:

$$F = \frac{MS_{\text{between treatments}}}{MS_{\text{within}}} = \frac{\text{treatment effect} + \text{error (including individual differences)}}{\text{error (including individual differences)}}$$

In this formula, when the treatment effect is zero (H_0 true), the expected F ratio is one.

In the repeated-measures study, however, there are no individual differences between treatments because the same individuals are tested in every treatment. This means that variability due to individual differences is *not* a component of the numerator of the F ratio. Therefore, the individual differences must also be removed from the denominator of the F ratio to maintain a balanced ratio with an expected value of 1.00 when there is no treatment effect. That is, we want the repeated-measures F-ratio to have the following structure:

$$F = \frac{\text{treatment effect} + \text{error (without individual differences)}}{\text{error (with individual differences removed)}}$$

This is accomplished by a two-stage analysis. In the first stage, total variability (SS_{total}) is partitioned into the between-treatments SS and within-treatments SS. (Note, this is the same process we used for the independent-measures ANOVA.) In the second stage of the analysis, we measure the individual differences by computing the variability between subjects. This value is subtracted from SS_{within} leaving a remainder or residual variability due to experimental error. This two stage process is outlined in Figure 14.1 of your text.

One of the main advantages of the repeated-measures design is that the role of individual differences can be eliminated from the study. This advantage can be very important in situations where large individual differences would otherwise obscure the treatment effect in an independent-measures study.

Two-Factor Designs

Chapter 14 also extends analysis of variance to research designs that involve two independent variables. In the context of ANOVA, an independent variable (or a quasi-independent variable) is called a **factor**, and research studies with two factors are called **factorial designs** or simply **two-factor designs**. The two factors are identified as A and B, and the structure of a two-factor design can be represented as a matrix with the levels of factor A determining the rows and the levels of factor B determining the columns. For example, a researcher studying the effectiveness of three different teaching methods for three different class sizes could use the following experimental design:

	B1 Small class	B2 Average class	B3 Large class
A1 Method I	Sample 1	Sample 2	Sample 3
A2 Method II	Sample 4	Sample 5	Sample 6

Notice that the study involves two levels of teaching method and three levels of class size, creating a two-by-three matrix with a total of 6 different treatment conditions. Each treatment condition is represented by a cell in the matrix. For an independent-measures research study, a separate sample would be used for each of the six conditions.

Main Effects and Interactions

The goal for the two-factor ANOVA is to determine whether the mean differences that are observed for the sample data are sufficiently large to conclude that they are *significant* differences and not simply the result of sampling error. For the example we are considering, the goal is to determine whether different teaching methods and different class sizes produce significant differences in performance. To evaluate the sample mean differences, a two-factor ANOVA conducts three separate and independent hypothesis tests. The three tests evaluate:

1. **The Main Effect for Factor A** The mean differences between the levels of factor A are obtained by computing the overall mean for each row in the matrix. In this example, the main effect of factor A would compare the overall mean performance for Method I versus the overall mean performance for Method II.

2. **The Main Effect for Factor B** The mean differences between the levels of factor B are obtained by computing the overall mean for each column in the matrix. In this example, the ANOVA would compare the overall mean performance for small versus average versus large classes.

3. **The A x B Interaction** Often two factors will "interact" so that specific combinations of the two factors produce results (mean differences) that are not explained by the overall effects of either factor. For example, one teaching method may be very effective for small classes but not as effective for large classes. In this case, unique combinations of teaching method and class size produce results that are not explained by the overall main effects. These "extra" mean differences are the interaction.

The primary advantage of combining two factors (independent variables) in a single research study is that it allows you to examine how the two factors interact with each other. That is, the results will not only show the overall main effects of each factor, but also how unique combinations of the two variables may produce unique results. The interaction can be defined as "extra" mean differences, beyond the main effects of the two factors. An alternative definition is that an interaction exists when the effects of one factor depend on the levels of the second factor.

The Two-Factor Analysis of Variance

The two-factor ANOVA can be viewed as a two stage process. The first stage of the analysis is identical to the single-factor ANOVA (Chapter 13) and separates the total variability (SS and df) into two basic components: between treatments and within treatments. Each cell in the matrix is considered a separate treatment condition.

The second stage of the analysis separates the between-treatments variability into the three components that will form the numerators for the three F-ratios: Variance due to factor A, variance due to factor B, and variance due to the AxB interaction.

LEARNING OBJECTIVES

1. Be able to explain the logic of the repeated-measures ANOVA and be able to conduct a repeated-measures analysis to evaluate the mean differences from a repeated-measures study comparing two or more treatment conditions.

2. Know the differences between the analysis for repeated- versus independent-measures designs.

3. Be able to conduct a two-factor ANOVA to evaluate the data from an independent-measures experiment that uses two independent variables.

4. Understand the definitions of a main effect for one factor and an interaction between two factors, and be able to recognize an interaction from a description or a graph of experimental results.

NEW TERMS AND CONCEPTS

The following terms were introduced in this chapter. You should be able to define or describe each term and, where appropriate, describe how each term is related to other terms in the list.

between-treatments variability	The differences that exist from one treatment to another (a measure of mean differences).
within-treatments variability	The differences that exist inside each treatment condition.
between-subjects variability	The differences that exist from one subject to another.
error variability	Unexplained, unsystematic differences that are not caused by any known factor.
treatment effect	Systematic differences that are caused by changing treatment conditions.
individual differences	Consistent differences that exist between one individual and another.
F-ratio	A ratio of two variances: between-treatments variance in the numerator and chance/error in the denominator.
two-factor study	A research study examining two factors (two independent or quasi-independent variables).
main effect	The overall mean differences between the levels of one factor. When the data are organized in a matrix, the main effects are the mean differences among the rows (or among the columns).
interaction	Mean differences that cannot be explained by the main effects of the two factors. An interaction exists when the effects of one factor depend on the levels of the second factor.

NEW FORMULAS

In addition to the total SS, between-treatments SS, within-treatments SS, and the corresponding df and MS values that were presented in Chapter 13, several new formulas are introduced in Chapter 14:

Repeated-Measures ANOVA

$$SS_{\text{between subjects}} = \Sigma \frac{P^2}{k} - \frac{G^2}{N}$$

$$df_{\text{between subjects}} = n - 1$$

$$SS_{\text{error}} = SS_{\text{within}} - SS_{\text{between subjects}}$$

$$df_{\text{error}} = df_{\text{within}} - df_{\text{between subjects}}$$

$$= (N - k) - (n - 1)$$

Two-Factor ANOVA

$$SS_{\text{factor A}} = \Sigma \frac{T^2_{\text{ROW}}}{n_{\text{ROW}}} - \frac{G^2}{N} \qquad df_{\text{factor A}} = (\text{number levels of A}) - 1$$

$$SS_{\text{factor B}} = \Sigma \frac{T^2_{\text{COL}}}{n_{\text{COL}}} - \frac{G^2}{N} \qquad df_{\text{factor B}} = (\text{number levels of B}) - 1$$

$$SS_{\text{AxB}} = SS_{\text{bet cells}} - SS_A - SS_B \qquad df_{\text{AxB}} = df_{\text{bet. cells}} - df_A - df_B$$

STEP BY STEP

The repeated-measures ANOVA is used to determine whether there are significant differences among the means of two or more different treatments, using the data from a single sample that has been measured in each treatment condition. The calculations and notation for the repeated-measures ANOVA are very similar to the independent-measures design. In fact, the first stage of the repeated-measures analysis is identical to the independent ANOVA. However, the repeated analysis continues through a second stage where the individual differences are removed from the denominator of the F-ratio. The following example will be used to demonstrate the repeated-measures ANOVA.

A researcher is comparing four different treatment conditions using a repeated-measures experiment with a sample of n = 6 subjects. The data from this experiment are as follows:

Subject	Treatment 1	2	3	4	P
#1	0	2	6	0	8
#2	4	0	7	1	12
#3	5	4	11	0	20
#4	8	7	13	4	32
#5	7	2	9	2	20
#6	6	3	14	5	28
T	30	18	60	12	
SS	40	28	52	22	

$G = 120$

$\Sigma X^2 = 970$

Step 1: State the hypotheses and select an alpha level. The null hypothesis states that there are no differences among the means for the four treatment conditions.

$$H_0: \ \mu_1 = \mu_2 = \mu_3 = \mu_4$$

The general alternative hypothesis is,
H_1: At least one of the treatment means is different from another.
We will use $\alpha = .05$.

Step 2: Locate the critical region. The first problem is to determine the df values for the F-ratio. We will conduct a complete analysis of df to determine the values for $df_{between\ treatments}$ and df_{error}. For these data,

$df_{total} = N - 1 = 24 - 1 = 23$
$df_{between\ treatments} = k - 1 = 4 - 1 = 3$
$df_{within\ treatments} = N - k = 24 - 4 = 20$

This completes the first stage of the analysis. (Check to be sure that the total equals the sum of the two components.) For the second stage,

$$df_{\text{between subjects}} = n - 1 = 6 - 1 = 5$$

$$
\begin{aligned}
df_{\text{error}} &= df_{\text{within}} - df_{\text{between subjects}} \\
&= 20 - 5 \\
&= 15
\end{aligned}
$$

The F-ratio will have df = 3, 15. For α = .05 the critical F value is 3.29. Any value larger than 3.29 will result in rejecting the null hypotheisi.

Step 3: Compute the test statistic. We have completed the analysis for df, so we will continue with the analysis of SS. As before, we will complete the analysis in two stages. The first stage is identical to the independent-measures ANOVA and produces:

$$SS_{\text{total}} = \Sigma X^2 - \frac{G^2}{N} = 370$$

$$SS_{\text{between treatments}} = \Sigma \frac{T^2}{n} - \frac{G^2}{N} = 228$$

$$SS_{\text{within}} = \Sigma SS = 40 + 28 + 52 + 22 = 142$$

This completes the first stage. (Check to be sure that the two components add to the total.) Continuing with the second stage,

$$
\begin{aligned}
SS_{\text{subjects}} &= \Sigma \frac{P^2}{k} - \frac{G^2}{N} \\
&= \frac{8^2}{4} + \frac{12^2}{4} + \frac{20^2}{4} + \frac{32^2}{4} + \frac{20^2}{4} + \frac{28^2}{4} - \frac{120^2}{24} \\
&= 704 - 600 = 104
\end{aligned}
$$

$$
\begin{aligned}
SS_{\text{error}} &= SS_{\text{within}} - SS_{\text{subjects}} \\
&= 142 - 104 = 38
\end{aligned}
$$

Next, compute the two mean squares (MS values) that will form the F- ratio.

$$MS_{between\ treatments} = \frac{SS_{between\ treatments}}{df_{between\ treatments}} = 228/3 = 76$$

$$MS_{error} = \frac{SS_{error}}{df_{error}} = 38/15 = 2.53$$

Finally, the F-ratio for these data is,

$$F = \frac{MS_{between\ treatments}}{MS_{error}} = 76/2.53 = 30.04$$

Step 4: Make decision. The F-ratio for these data is in the critical region. This is a very unlikely value to be obtained if H_0 is true. Therefore, we reject H_0 and conclude that there are significant differences among the four treatment means.

Two-Factor ANOVA: The two-factor analysis of variance is used to evaluate mean differences in a research study that uses two independent variables or two quasi-independent variables . The two factors are generally identified as A and B, and the data are presented in a matrix with the levels of factor A determining the rows and the levels of factor B determining the columns. The analysis of variance evaluates three separate hypotheses: one concerning the main effect of factor A, one concerning the main effect of factor B, and one concerning the interaction. In this chapter we considered the two-factor analysis for an independent-measures research study which means that the data consist of a separate sample for each AB treatment combination. The following example will be used to demonstrate the two-factor ANOVA.

The following data are from a two-factor experiment with 2 levels of factor A and 3 levels of factor B. There are n = 10 subjects in each treatment condition.

	B1	B2	B3	
A1	T = 10 SS = 20	T = 20 SS = 32	T = 30 SS = 35	$T_{A1} = 60$
A2	T = 10 SS = 15	T = 10 SS = 35	T = 10 SS = 25	$T_{A2} = 30$

$T_{B1} = 20 \qquad T_{B2} = 30 \qquad T_{B3} = 40$

$G = 90$
$\Sigma X^2 = 332$

Step 1: State the hypotheses and select an alpha level. Because the two-factor ANOVA evaluates three separate hypotheses, there will be three null hypotheses.

For Factor A: H_0: $\mu_{A1} = \mu_{A2}$ (no A-effect)
$\qquad\qquad$ H_1: $\mu_{A1} \neq \mu_{A2}$

For Factor B: H_0: $\mu_{B1} = \mu_{B2} = \mu_{B3}$ (no B-effect)
$\qquad\qquad$ H_1: At least one of the B means is different from another.

For AxB: H_0: There is no interaction between factors A and B. That is, the effect of either factor does not depend on the levels of the other factor.
$\qquad\quad$ H_1: There is an A x B interaction.

We will use $\alpha = .05$ for all three tests.

Step 2: Locate the critical regions. Because there are three separate tests, each with its own F-ratio, we will need to determine the critical region for each test separately. All three F-ratios use MS as the denominator (error term) and
$\qquad df_{within} = \Sigma(n - 1) = 9 + 9 + 9 + 9 + 9 + 9 = 54$
Thus, factor A will have an F-ratio with df = 1, 54. Factor B and the AxB interaction both will have F- ratios with df = 2, 54. For factor A, with $\alpha = .05$, the critical value is 4.02. For factor B and for the interaction, with $\alpha = .05$, the critical value is 3.17. (Because df = 54 is not listed, we have used 55 for the denominator in each case.)

Step 3: Calculate the test statistic. The analysis proceeds in two stages. The first stage is identical to the single-factor analysis (Chapter 13) and divides the total variability into two components, between-treatments and within-treatments, with each cell considered as a separate treatment condition. For these data,

$$SS_{total} = \Sigma X^2 - \frac{G^2}{N} = 197 \qquad df_{total} = 59$$

$$SS_{bet.\ cells} = \Sigma \frac{T^2}{n} - \frac{G^2}{N} = 35 \qquad df_{bet..\ cells} = 5$$

$$SS_{within} = \Sigma SS = 162 \qquad df_{within} = 54$$

For the second stage,

$$SS_{factor\ A} = \Sigma \frac{T^2_{ROW}}{n_{ROW}} - \frac{G^2}{N} = \frac{60^2}{30} + \frac{30^2}{30} - \frac{90^2}{60} = 15 \qquad df_A = 1$$

$$SS_{factor\ B} = \Sigma \frac{T^2_{COL}}{n_{COL}} - \frac{G^2}{N} = \frac{20^2}{20} + \frac{30^2}{20} + \frac{40^2}{20} - \frac{90^2}{60} = 10 \qquad df_B = 2$$

$$SS_{A\times B} = SS_{bet\ cells} - SS_A - SS_B = 10 \qquad df_{A\times B} = 2$$

Next, compute the MS values that will become the numerators for the three F-ratios.

$$MS_A = \frac{SS_A}{df_A} = 15/1 = 15 \qquad MS_B = \frac{SS_B}{df_B} = 10/2 = 5$$

$$MS_{AxB} = \frac{SS_{AxB}}{df_{AxB}} = 10/2 = 5$$

All three F-ratios will have the same error term denominator:

$$MS_{within} = \frac{SS_{within}}{df_{within}} = 162/54 = 3$$

Finally, the three F-ratios are,

For Factor A: $F = \dfrac{MS_A}{MS_{within}} = 15/3 = 5.00$

For Factor B: $F = \dfrac{MS_B}{MS_{within}} = 5/3 = 1.67$

For AxB: $F = \dfrac{MS_{AxB}}{MS_{within}} = 5/3 = 1.67$

Step 4: Make decision. The F-ratio for Factor A is in the critical region. Therefore, we reject this H_0 and conclude that there is a significant difference between the mean for A1 and the mean for A2. The F-ratios for factor B and for the AxB interaction are not in the critical region. Therefore, we conclude that there is no significant main effect for factor B, and the data are not sufficient to conclude that there is an interaction between factors A and B.

HINTS AND CAUTIONS

1. One important fact that may help you to remember the structure and the value of a repeated-measures ANOVA is that the repeated-measures design eliminates individual differences. The individual differences do not exist in the numerator of the F-ratio because the same individuals are used in all of the treatment conditions. In the denominator of the F-ratio there are no individual differences because they are subtracted out in the second stage of the analysis.

2.   For a two-factor ANOVA, remember that the F-ratios for factor A, factor B, and the AxB interaction can all have different values for df and therefore may have different critical values. Be sure that you use the appropriate critical region for each individual F-ratio.

SELF TEST
True/False Questions

1. For a repeated-measures design, the differences between treatments may be caused by a treatment effect or by chance/error, but they cannot be caused by individual differences.

2. In the second stage of analysis for the repeated-measures ANOVA, the within-treatments variability is partitioned into $SS_{between\ subjects}$ and SS_{error}.

3. If there are large individual differences among subjects, an independent-measures study will be more sensitive than a repeated-measures study in detecting a treatment effect.

4. For the repeated-measures analysis, the F-ratio, on average, is expected to be zero when H_0 is true.

5. The result of a repeated-measures ANOVA stated that $F(4, 20) = 11.57$, $p < .01$. The study had 4 treatment conditions.

6. A "factorial" experimental design means that the research study contains at least two dependent variables.

7. A two-factor analysis of variance with 2 levels of factor A and 3 levels of factor B involves six separate hypothesis tests.

8. In a two-factor ANOVA, all of the F-ratios use the same denominator.

9. A researcher predicts that a special training course will be equally effective for males and females. This researcher is predicting an interaction between training and gender.

10. In a two-factor ANOVA, a significant interaction means that one of the factors has a significant effect but the second factor does not.

Multiple-Choice Questions

1. Which of the following accurately describes the two stages of a repeated-measures analysis of variance?
   - a. The first stage is identical to the independent-measures analysis and the second stage removes individual differences from the numerator of the F-ratio.
   - b. The first stage is identical to the independent-measures analysis and the second stage removes individual differences from the denominator of the F-ratio.
   - c. The first stage removes individual differences from the numerator of the F-ratio and the second stage is identical to the independent-measures analysis.
   - d. The first stage removes individual differences from the denominator of the F-ratio and the second stage is identical to the independent-measures analysis.

2. In the repeated-measures ANOVA, individual differences are *not* a source of variability for between treatment SS because _____.
   - a this factor is mathematically subtracted for between treatment SS
   - b. the same subjects serve in every treatment condition
   - c. individual differences in the numerator and denominator of the F ratio cancel each other
   - d. None of the other 3 choices is correct.

3. The results of a repeated-measures ANOVA indicate that the within-treatment SS is 12 and the between-subject SS is 4. For this analysis, error SS is _____.
   - a. 8
   - b. 16
   - c. 48
   - d. insufficient information to find error SS

4. In Stage 2 of the repeated-measures ANOVA, within treatments degrees of freedom is partitioned into _____.
   - a. between treatments df and error df
   - b. between subjects df and error df
   - c. between treatments df and between subjects df
   - d. total df and error df

5. A repeated-measures analysis of variance with a sample of n = 8 participants, produces $df_{\text{within treatments}}$ = 14. What is the value for df_{error} for this analysis?

    a. 6
    b. 7
    c. 21
    d. cannot determine without additional information

6. A researcher reports an F-ratio with df = 3, 21 from a repeated-measures ANOVA. How many treatment conditions were compared in this experiment?

    a. 3
    b. 4
    c. 22
    d. 24

7. A researcher reports an F-ratio with df = 3, 21 from a repeated-measures ANOVA. How many subjects participated in this experiment?

    a. 4
    b. 8
    c. 24
    d. 32

8. In a repeated-measures ANOVA, which of the following is not computed directly but rather is obtained by a process of subtraction?

    a. $SS_{\text{Between Subjects}}$
    b. $SS_{\text{Within Treatments}}$
    c. $SS_{\text{Between Treatments}}$
    d. SS_{Error}

9. A two-factor study with two levels of factor A and three levels of factor B uses a separate group of n = 5 participants in each treatment condition. How many participants are needed for the entire study?

    a. 5
    b. 10
    c. 25
    d. 30

10. In an experiment with 2 levels of factor A, 3 levels of factor B, and $n = 5$ in each treatment condition, what is the correct value for the degrees of freedom within treatments?
   a. 30
   b. 29
   c. 24
   d. 8

11. A significant interaction between factors A and B indicates _____.
   a. either the main effect for factor A or the main effect for factor B is also significant, but not both
   b. both the main effect for factor A and for factor B must also be significant
   c. neither of the two main effects is significant
   d. The significance of the interaction has no implications for the main effects.

12. The results of a two-factor analysis of variance produce $SS_{bet.\ cells} = 20$ and $SS_{within} = 10$. The analysis also produces $SS_A = 5$ and $SS_B = 3$. Based on this information, the value of SS_{AxB} would be _____.
   a. 8
   b. 10
   c. 12
   d. 28

13. The following data represent the means for each treatment condition in a two-factor experiment. Note that one mean is not given. What value for the missing mean would result in no main effect for factor A?
   a. 10
   b. 20
   c. 30
   d. 40

	B1	B2
A1	20	30
A2	40	?

14. The following data represent the means for each treatment condition in a two-factor experiment. Note that one mean is not given. What value for the missing mean would result in no AxB interaction?

a. 10
b. 20
c. 30
d. 40

	B1	B2
A1	20	10
A2	40	?

15. If the mean and variance are computed for each sample in an independent-measures two-factor experiment, then which of the following types of sample data will tend to produce large F-ratios for the two-factor ANOVA?

a. large differences between sample means and small sample variances
b. large differences between sample means and large sample variances
c. small differences between sample means and small sample variances
d. small differences between sample means and large sample variances

Other Questions

1. A toy manufacturer is testing 3 versions of a toy that is under development. Among other things, the manufacturer would like to see which version of the toy attracts the most attention. A psychologist allows a child to play with all 3 toys and records the amount of time (in minutes) spent playing with each. A sample of n = 5 children is used. Use the following data to determine whether there is a significant preference among the three toys. Use the .05 level of significance.

Child	1	2	3
A	0	2	4
B	2	2	8
C	3	1	5
D	0	3	6
E	0	2	7

Toy

2. A sample of n = 7 individuals is selected to participate in a learning study. Each individual is tested at five different stages during learning (after 1 hour, 2 hours, 3 hours, etc.). The data from this experiment were examined using a repeated-measures ANOVA to determine whether there was any evidence of a practice effect. The results

are presented in the following summary table. Complete all the missing values in the
table. Hint: Begin with the df column.

Source	SS	df	MS	
Between Treatments	___	___	10	F = ___
Within Treatments	___	___		
Between Subjects	52	___		
Error	___	___	___	
Total	140	___		

3. Use a two-factor analysis of variance to evaluate the following data from an
independent-measures experimental design using $n = 5$ subjects for each treatment
condition (each cell). Use $\alpha = .05$ for all tests.

	B1	B2	B3
A1	M = 1 T = 5 SS = 15	M = 1 T = 5 SS = 15	M = 4 T = 20 SS = 25
A2	M = 1 T = 5 SS = 15	M = 3 T = 15 SS = 25	M = 8 T = 40 SS = 25

$$N = 30$$
$$G = 90$$
$$\Sigma X^2 = 580$$

ANSWERS TO SELF TEST

True/False Answers

1. True.
2. True
3. False. Repeated-measures is more sensitive because it reduces variance by
removing individual differences.
4. False. The F-ratio is structured to be balanced (F = 1.00) if the null
hypothesis is true.
5. False. With between-treatments df = 4, there must be 5 treatments.

6. False. A factorial study contains at least 2 independent variables.
7. False. A two-factor study requires 3 hypothesis tests (2 main effects and 1 interaction).
8. True
9. False. The effectiveness of the course does *not* depend on gender.
10. False. The significance of the interaction is completely independent of the significance of the main effects.

Multiple-Choice Answers

1. b   Because the same individuals are in every treatment, there are no individual differences between treatments, however, the individual differences must be subtracted from the denominator of the F-ratio.
2. b   The same individuals participate in all treatments, so differences between treatment cannot be explained by differences between participants.
3. a   Error = Within treatment – between subjects.
4. b   In stage 2, the individual differences (between subjects) are separated from the error.
5. b   error df = within-treatments df – between subjects df.
6. b   With df between = 3, there must be 4 tratements.
7. b   With 8 individuals in each of 4 treatments, k - 1 = 3, and (N - k) - (n - 1) = 28 - 7 = 21.
8. d   SS error is the remainder when individual differences are subtracted from SS within treatments.
9. d   There are 2x3 = 6 different treatments, each with n = 5 participants.
10. c   There are 2x3 = 6 treatments, each with n – 1 = 4 degrees of freedom.
11. d   The significance of the interaction is independent of the main effects.
12. c   SS for the interaction is the remainder after the A and B effects have been subtracted from the SS between cells.
13. a   If the missing value is 10 then both rows (A1 and A2) average 25.
14. c   In the top row the mean drops by 10 (from 20 to 10). If there is no interaction, the bottom row should show the same pattern.
15. a   Large mean differences lead to large numerators for F, and small variance lead to small denominators.

Other Answers

1. The null hypothesis states that there are no differences among the 3 toys. With df = 2,8, the critical boundary is F = 4.46.

Source	SS	df	MS	
Between Treatments	70	2	35	F = 20
Within Treatments	20	12		
Between Subjects	6	4		
Error	14	8	1.75	
Total	90	14		

Reject the null hypothesis and conclude that there are significant differences among the three toys.

2.

Source	SS	df	MS	
Between Treatments	40	4	10	F = 5.00
Within Treatments	100	30		
Between Subjects	52	6		
Error	48	24	2	
Total	140	34		

3. The results of the two-factor ANOVA are summarized as follows:

Source	SS	df	MS	
Between Cells	190	5		
Factor A	30	1	30	F(1, 24) = 6.00
Factor B	140	2	70	F(2, 24) = 14.00
AxB	20	2	10	F(2, 24) = 2.00
Within Cells	120	24	5	
Total	310	29		

For df = 1, 24 the critical value is 4.26. The F-ratio for factor A is in the critical region so there is a significant difference among the levels of factor A. With df = 2, 24 the critical value is 3.40. The F-ratio for factor B is in the critical region so there are significant differences among the levels of factor B. The interaction is not significant.

CHAPTER 15

CORRELATION AND REGRESSION

CHAPTER SUMMARY

The goals of Chapter 15 are:
1. To introduce the concept of a correlation and what it measures.
2. To demonstrate the Pearson correlation to measure linear relationship.
3. To demonstrate the Spearman correlation to measure relationships for ordinal data.
4. To demonstrate the Point-Biserial Correlation and the Phi-Coefficient.
5. To introduce the process of linear regression.
6. To demonstrate the analysis of regression to evaluate the significance of a linear regression equation.

Correlations: Measuring and Describing Relationships

A correlation is a statistical method used to measure and describe the relationship between two variables. A relationship exists when changes in one variable tend to be accompanied by consistent and predictable changes in the other variable.

A correlation typically evaluates three aspects of the relationship: the direction, the form, and the degree of relationship. The **direction** of the relationship is measured by the sign of the correlation (+ or -). A positive correlation means that the two variables tend to change in the same direction; as one increases, the other also tends to increase. A negative correlation means that the two variables tend to change in opposite directions; as one increases, the other tends to decrease. The most common **form** of relationship is a straight line or linear relationship which is measured by the Pearson correlation. The **degree** of relationship (the strength or consistency of the relationship) is measured by the numerical value of the correlation. A value of 1.00 indicates a perfect relationship and a value of zero indicates no relationship.

To compute a correlation you need two scores, X and Y, for each individual in the sample. The Pearson correlation requires that the scores be numerical values from an interval or ratio scale of measurement. Other correlational methods exist for other scales of measurement.

The Pearson Correlation

The **Pearson correlation** measures the direction and degree of linear (straight line) relationship between two variables. To compute the Pearson correlation, you first measure the variability of X and Y scores separately by computing SS for the scores of each variable (SS_X and SS_Y). Then, the covariability (tendency for X and Y to vary together) is measured by the sum of products (SP). The Pearson correlation is found by computing the ratio, $SP/\sqrt{(SS_X)(SS_Y)}$. Thus the Pearson correlation is comparing the amount of covariability (variation from the relationship between X and Y) to the amount X and Y vary separately. The magnitude of the Pearson correlation ranges from 0 (indicating no linear relationship between X and Y) to 1.00 (indicating a perfect straight-line relationship between X and Y). The correlation can be either positive or negative depending on the direction of the relationship.

The Spearman Correlation

The **Spearman correlation** is used in two general situations: (1) It measures the relationship between two ordinal variables; that is, X and Y both consist of ranks. (2) It measures the consistency of direction of the relationship between two variables. In this case, the two variables must be converted to ranks before the Spearman correlation is computed. The calculation of the Spearman correlation requires:

1. Two variables are observed for each individual.

2. The observations for each variable are rank ordered. Note that the X values and the Y values are ranked separately.

3. After the variables have been ranked, the Spearman correlation is computed by either:
   a. Using the Pearson formula with the ranked data.
   b. Using the special Spearman formula (assuming there are few, if any, tied ranks).

The Point-Biserial Correlation and the Phi Coefficient

The Pearson correlation formula can also be used to measure the relationship between two variables when one or both of the variables is dichotomous. A dichotomous variable is one for which there are exactly two categories: for example, men/women or succeed/fail. With either one or two dichotomous variables the calculation of the correlation precedes as follows:
   1. Assign numerical values to the two categories of the dichotomous variable(s). Traditionally, one category is assigned a value of 0 and the other is assigned a value of 1.

2. Use the regular Pearson correlation formula to calculate the correlation.

In situations where one variable is dichotomous and the other consists of regular numerical scores (interval or ratio scale), the resulting correlation is called a **point-biserial correlation**. When both variables are dichotomous, the resulting correlation is called a **phi-coefficient**.

The point-biserial correlation is closely related to the independent-measures t test introduced in Chapter 10. When the data consists of one dichotomous variable and one numerical variable, the dichotomous variable can also be used to separate the individuals into two groups. Then, it is possible to compute a sample mean for the numerical scores in each group. In this case, the independent-measures t test can be used to evaluate the mean difference between groups. If the effect size for the mean difference is measured by computing r^2 (the percentage of variance explained), the value of r^2 will be equal to the value obtained by squaring the point-biserial correlation.

Introduction to Linear Regression

The Pearson correlation measures the degree to which a set of data points form a straight line relationship. **Regression** is a statistical procedure that determines the equation for the straight line that best fits a specific set of data.

Any straight line can be represented by an equation of the form $Y = bX + a$, where b and a are constants. The value of b is called the slope constant and determines the direction and degree to which the line is tilted. The value of a is called the Y-intercept and determines the point where the line crosses the Y-axis.

How well a set of data points fits a straight line can be measured by calculating the distance between the data points and the line. The total error between the data points and the line is obtained by squaring each distance and then summing the squared values. The regression equation is designed to produce the minimum sum of squared errors. The equation for the regression line is

$$\hat{Y} = bX + a \qquad \text{where } b = \frac{SP}{SS_X} \qquad \text{and} \qquad a = M_Y - bM_X$$

The ability of the regression equation to accurately predict the Y values is measured by first computing the proportion of the Y-score variability that is predicted by the regression equation and the proportion that is not predicted.

Predicted variability $= SS_{regression} = r^2 SS_Y$ with df $= 1$

Unpredicted variability $= SS_{resicual} = (1 - r^2)SS_Y = \Sigma(Y - \hat{Y})^2$ with df $= n - 2$

The unpredicted variability can be used to compute the standard error of estimate which is a measure of the average distance between the actual Y values and the predicted Y values.

$$\text{standard error of estimate} = \frac{SS_{residual}}{df}$$

Finally, the overall significance of the regression equation can be evaluated by computing an F-ratio. A significant F-ratio indicates that the equation predicts a significant portion of the variability in the Y scores (more than would be expected by chance alone). To compute the F-ratio, you first calculate a variance or MS for the predicted variability and for the unpredicted variability:

$$MS_{regressiion} = \frac{SS_{regression}}{df_{regression}} \quad \text{and} \quad MS_{residuals} = \frac{SS_{residuals}}{df_{residuals}}$$

The F-ratio is

$$F = \frac{MS_{regressiion}}{MS_{residuals}} \quad \text{with df} = 1, n - 2$$

LEARNING OBJECTIVES

1. Understand the Pearson correlation and what aspects of a relationship it measures.

2. Be able to compute the Pearson correlation by the regular formula (using either the definitional or computational formula for SP) or by the z-score formula.

3. Be able to use a sample correlation to evaluate a hypothesis about the correlation for the general population.

4. Understand the Spearman correlation and how it differs from the Pearson correlation in terms of the data it uses and the type of relationship it measures.

5. Understand how the Pearson correlation formula can be used to compute a point-biserial correlation or a phi-coefficient to measure the relationship between two variables when one or both variables are dichotomous.

6. Recognize the general form of a linear equation and be able to identify its slope and Y-intercept.

7. Be able to compute the linear regression equation for a set of data.

8. Be able to evaluate the significance of a linear regression equation by computing the appropriate F-ratio.

NEW TERMS AND CONCEPTS

The following terms were introduced in this chapter. You should be able to define or describe each term and, where appropriate, describe how each term is related to other terms in the list.

positive relationship	A relationship between two variables where increases in one variable tend to be accompanied by increases in the other variable.
negative relationship	A relationship between two variables where increases in one variable tend to be accompanied by decreases in the other variable.
perfect relationship	A relationship where the actual data points perfectly fit the specific form being measured. For a Pearson correlation, the data points fit perfectly on a straight line.
sum of products (of deviations)	A measure of the degree of covariability between two variables; the degree to which they vary together.
Pearson correlation	A measure of the direction and degree of linear relationship between two variables.

significance of a correlation	A demonstration that a sample correlation so large that it is very unlikely ($p < \alpha$) to have come from a population where the correlation is zero.
coefficient of determination	The degree to the variability in one variable can be predicted by its relationship with another variable: measured by r^2.
Spearman correlation	A correlation calculated for ordinal data. Also used to measure the consistency of direction for a relationship.
monotonic relation	A relationship that is consistently one-directional.
point-biserial correlation	A correlation between two variables where one of the variables is dichotomous.
phi-coefficient	A correlation between two variables both of which are dichotomous
linear equation	An equation of the form $Y = bX + a$ expressing the relationship between two variables X and Y.
slope	The amount of change in Y for each 1-point increase in X. The value of b in the linear equation.
Y-intercept	The value of Y when $X = 0$. In the linear equation, the value of a.
regression equation for Y	The equation for the best-fitting straight line to describe the relationship between X and Y.
predicted variability of Y	The proportion of the variability for the Y scores that is predicted by the regression equation. Determined by r^2 for linear regression.
unpredicted variability of Y	The proportion of the variability for the Y scores that is not predicted by the regression equation. (Also known as the residual variability.) Determined by $1 - r^2$ for linear regression.

standard error of estimate	A measure of the standard (average) distance between the actual Y values and the predicted values from the regression equation.
analysis of regression	Evaluating the significance of a regression equation by computing an F-ratio comparing the predicted variance (MS) in the numerator and the unpredicted variance (MS) in the denominator.

NEW FORMULAS

$$SP = \Sigma XY - \frac{(\Sigma X)(\Sigma Y)}{n} \quad \text{or} \quad SP = \Sigma(X - M_X)(Y - M_Y)$$

$$r = \frac{SP}{\sqrt{(SS_X)(SS_Y)}}$$

$$\text{Spearman } r_S = 1 - \frac{6\Sigma D^2}{n(n^2 - 1)}$$

$$\hat{Y} = bX + a \qquad b = \frac{SP}{SS_X} \qquad a = M_Y - bM_X$$

$$SS_{regression} = r^2 SS_Y \qquad df = 1 \qquad MS_{regression} = SS/df$$

$$SS_{residual} = (1 - r^2)SS_Y \quad df = n - 2 \qquad MS_{residual} = SS/df$$

$$F = \frac{MS_{regression}}{MS_{residual}}$$

STEP BY STEP

The Pearson Correlation A researcher has pairs of scores (X and Y values) for a sample of $n = 5$ subjects. The data are as follows:

Person	X	Y
#1	0	−2
#2	2	−5
#3	8	14
#4	6	3
#5	4	0

Step 1: Sketch a scatter plot of the data and make a preliminary estimate of the correlation.

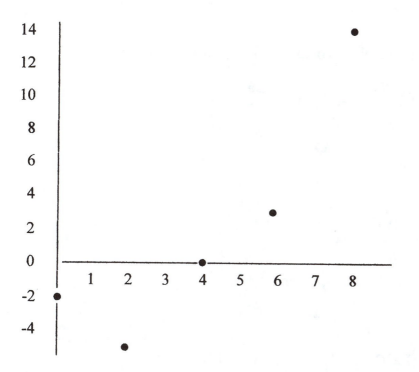

For these data, there appears to be a fairly good, positive correlation - probably around $r = +.8$ or $+.9$.

Step 2: To compute the Pearson correlation you must find SS for both X and Y as well as SP. If both sets of scores (X and Y) have means that are whole numbers, then you may use the definitional formulas for SS and SP. Otherwise, it is better to use the computational formulas. Although these data have $M_X = 4$ and $M_Y = 2$, we will demonstrate the computational formulas.

Using one large table, list the X and Y values in the first two columns, then continue with the squared values and the XY products. Find the sum of the

Using one large table, list the X and Y values in the first two columns, then continue with the squared values and the XY products. Find the sum of the numbers in each column. These sums are needed to find SS and SP.

X	Y	X^2	Y^2	XY
0	-2	0	4	0
2	-5	4	25	-10
8	14	64	196	112
6	3	36	9	18
4	0	16	0	0

(totals) 20 10 120 234 120

Use the sums from the table to compute SS for X and Y, and SP.

$$\text{For X: SS} = \Sigma X^2 - \frac{(\Sigma X)^2}{n} = 120 - \frac{20^2}{5}$$

$$= 120 - 80$$

$$= 40$$

$$\text{For Y: SS} = \Sigma Y^2 - \frac{(\Sigma Y)^2}{n} = 234 - \frac{10^2}{5}$$

$$= 234 - 20$$

$$= 214$$

$$\text{and SP} = \Sigma XY - \frac{(\Sigma X)(\Sigma Y)}{n} = 120 - \frac{(20)(10)}{5}$$

$$= 120 - 40$$

$$= 80$$

Step 3: Compute the Pearson correlation and compare the answer with your preliminary estimate from Step 1. For these data,

$$r = \frac{SP}{\sqrt{(SS_X)(SS_Y)}} = \frac{80}{\sqrt{(40)(214)}} = \frac{80}{92.52} = 0.865$$

The obtained correlation, $r = +0.865$ agrees with our preliminary estimate.

<u>Linear Regression</u>   We will find the regression equation for the same data that were used to demonstrate the Pearson correlation. The general form of the regression equation is, $\hat{Y} = bX + a$. For these data,

$$b = \frac{SP}{SS_X} = \frac{80}{40} = 2$$

and $a = a = M_Y - bM_X$

$\qquad\quad = 2 - 2(4)$

$\qquad\quad = -6$

The regression equation is: $\hat{Y} = 2X - 6$

Both the slope constant ($b = +2$) and the Y-intercept ($a = -6$) agree with the appearance of the points in the scatter plot.

<u>Analysis of Regression</u>   The significance of the regression equation can be evaluated using an analysis of regression. The null hypothesis says that there is no consistent relationship between X and Y in the population and the regression equation does not predict a significant portion of the variance for the Y scores.
  The analysis of regression is based on an F-ratio comparing the variance predicted by the equation and the unpredicted, or residual variance. The predicted portion of the variance is determined by r^2 and the unpredicted portion by $1 - r^2$. For the data we have been considering, $r = 0.865$ and $SS_Y = 214$. Using these values, we obtain

$$SS_{regression} = r^2 SS_Y = (0.865)^2(214) = 0.748(214) = 160.07$$

$$SS_{residual} = (1 - r^2)SS_Y = (1 - 0.748)(214) = 0.252(214) = 53.93$$

$$MS_{regression} = \frac{SS_{regression}}{df} = \frac{160.07}{1} = 160.07$$

$$MS_{residual} = \frac{SS_{residual}}{df} = \frac{53.93}{n-2} = \frac{53.93}{5-2} = 17.98$$

$$\text{and the F-ratio is, } F = \frac{MS_{regression}}{MS_{residual}} = \frac{160.07}{17.98} = 8.90$$

With df = 2, 3 and α = .05, the critical value is 9.55. The decision is to fail to reject the null hypothesis. Our conclusion is that the regression equation does not predict a significant portion of the variance for the Y scores.

HINTS AND CAUTIONS

1. Remember, a correlation of -0.80 is just as strong as a correlation of +0.80. The sign indicates the direction of the relationship, not its magnitude.

2. Remember that n refers to the number of individuals (pairs of scores).

3. The special formula for the Spearman correlation often causes trouble. Remember, the value of the fraction is computed separately and then subtracted from 1.00. The 1 is not a part of the fraction.

4. When computing either the point-biserial correlation or the phi-coefficient, the numerical values are assigned arbitrarily to the two dichotomous categories. As a result, the sign of the correlation (+ or n –) is also arbitrary and meaningless.

5. Although linear regression can be conducted without first computing a correlation, it is usually helpful to calculate the Pearson correlation, especially if you plan to evaluate the significance of the regression equation.

SELF TEST

True/False Questions

1. A negative correlation indicates that decreases in one variable tend to be accompanied by decreases in the other variable.

2. The value of sum of products (SP) can never be less than zero.

3. In a scatter plot, the more the data points vary from a straight line, the closer the value for the Pearson correlation is to zero.

4. For a Pearson correlation, the degree to which the data points fit on a straight line is measured by a numerical value ranging from 0 to 1.00.

5. A researcher observing children on a school playground noticed that the number of aggressive acts tends to increase as the temperature increases. This is an example of a positive correlation.

6. A Pearson correlation of +0.90 indicates that the data points are tightly clustered around a line sloping down to the right.

7. The Spearman correlation is used to measure the relationship when both variables have been measured on an ordinal scale (both are ranks).

8. The point-biserial correlation is used with data that also would be appropriate for an independent-measures t hypothesis test.

9. The proportion of SS_Y that is not predicted by the regression equation is equal to r^2.

10. For linear regression with one predictor variable, $SS_{regression}$ has df $= 1$ and $SS_{resdiual}$ has df $= n - 1$.

Multiple-Choice Questions

1. During the winter in New York, the lower the temperature drops, the higher the demand for energy. This is an example of
      a. a positive relationship.
      b. a negative relationship.
      c. a cause-effect relationship.
      d. all of the above.

2. Which of the following most completely describes the possible values for the Pearson correlation?
      a. $r \leq 1.00$
      b. $r \geq -1.00$
      c. $-1.00 \leq r \leq 1.00$
      d. $r \geq 0$

3. Which of the following Pearson correlations shows the greatest strength or consistency of relationship?
     a. -0.90
     b. +0.74
     c. +0.85
     d. -0.33

4. What pattern would appear in a graph of a Pearson correlation of $r = +0.80$?
     a. points tightly clustered around a line that slopes up to the right.
     b. points tightly clustered around a line that slopes down to the right.
     c. points widely scattered around a line that slopes up to the right.
     d. points widely scattered around a line that slopes down to the right.

5. A set of $n = 10$ pairs of scores has $\Sigma X = 20$, $\Sigma Y = 30$, and $\Sigma XY = 74$. What is the value of SP for these data?
     a. 74
     b. 24
     c. 14
     d. −14

6. A set of $n = 15$ pairs of scores (X and Y values) has $SS_X = 4$, $SS_Y = 16$, and $SP = 4$. The Pearson correlation for these data is
     a. $4/20 = 0.20$
     b. $4/64 = 0.0625$
     c. $4/\sqrt{20} = 0.89$
     d. $4/\sqrt{64} = 0.50$

7. A set of $n = 15$ pairs of scores (X and Y values) produces a correlation of $r = 0.40$. If each of the X values is multiplied by 2 and the correlation is computed for the new scores, what value will be obtained for the new correlation?
     a. $r = 0.20$
     b. $r = 0.40$
     c. $r = 0.80$
     d. cannot be determined without knowing all the X and Y scores

8. A researcher obtains a correlation of r = 0.40 for a sample of n = 25 pairs of scores. Which of the following correctly describes the significance of the correlation?
    a. It is not a significant correlation for either α = .05 or α = .01.
    b. It is a significant correlation for α = .05 but not for α = .01.
    c. It is a significant correlation for α = .01 but not for α = .05.
    d. It is a significant correlation for both α = .05 and α = .05.

9. When the Pearson correlation is computed for data measured on an ordinal scale (ranks), the result is know as
    a. the Spearman correlation.
    b. the point-biserial correlation.
    c. the phi coefficient.
    d. It is still called a Pearson correlation.

10. If the following seven scores are ranked from smallest (#1) to largest (#7) what rank should be assigned to a score of X = 4? Scores: 1, 4, 4, 5, 6, 6, 9
    a. 2
    b. 3
    c. either 2 or 3
    d. 2.5

11. Under what circumstances is the phi-coefficient used?
    a. When one variable consists of ranks and the other is regular, numerical scores.
    b. When both variables consists of ranks.
    c. When both X and Y are dichotomous variables
    d. When one variable is dichotomous and the other is regular, numerical scores.

12. What pattern would appear in a graph of the equation Y = 4X – 1.?
    a. a line that slopes steeply up to the right.
    b. a line that slopes steeply down to the right.
    c. a line that slopes gradually up to the right.
    d. a line that slopes gradually down to the right.

13. Assuming that SS_Y is constant, which of the following correlations would have the smallest $SS_{residual}$?
    a. r = -0.10
    b. r = +0.40
    c. r = -0.70
    d. There is no relationship between the correlation and $SS_{residual}$.

14. A linear regression equation has $b = 2$ and $a = 3$. What is the predicted value of Y for X = 8?

     a. $\hat{Y} = 5$
     b. $\hat{Y} = 19$
     c. $\hat{Y} = 26$
     d. cannot be determined without additional information

15. For a linear regression equation, the sum of the squared residuals can be computed directly by finding the difference between each Y and its predicted Y, then squaring the difference and adding the squared values. An alternative procedure is to calculate

     a. $r^2 SS_Y$
     b. $(1 - r^2)SS_Y$
     c. $(1 + r^2)SS_Y$
     d. SS_Y/SS_X

Other Questions

1. Compute SP for the following sets of data. You should find that the definitional formula works well with Set I because both means are whole numbers. However, the computational formula is better with Set II where the means are fractions.

Data Set I			Data Set II	
X	Y		X	Y
1	5		1	1
5	2		4	0
6	9		3	0
10	5		2	1
8	4			

2. For the following set of scores:
     a. Compute the Pearson correlation.
     b. Find the regression equation for predicting Y from X

X	Y
2	2
3	7
4	6
2	4
4	6

3.   Suppose that a sample of n = 18 pairs of X and Y scores yields a Pearson correlation of r = +0.40. Does this sample provide sufficient evidence to conclude that a significant correlation exists in the population? Test at the .05 level of significance, two tails.

4. Compute the point-biserial correlation for the following set of data. (Note that you will need to convert the Male/Female categories into 0/1 scores.

X	Y
Male	3
Female	7
Female	4
Male	7
Female	5
Male	2
Male	4
Female	8

5.   Suppose that a sample of n = 12 pairs of X and Y scores has SS_Y = 90 and a Pearson correlation of r = +0.40.
   a. What proportion of the variance for the Y scores is predicted by the regression equation?
   b. Does the regression equation predict a significant portion of the variance? Test with α = .05.

ANSWERS TO SELF TEST

True/False Answers

   1.   False. For a negative correlation, decreases in one variable tend to be accompanied by increases in the other variable.
   2. False. The value of SP can be either positive or negative.
   3. True
   4. True

   5. True

6. False. A line sloping down to the right indicates a negative correlation.
7. True
8. True
9. False. r^2 measures the predicted portion.
10. False. $SS_{residual}$ has df $= n - 2$

Multiple-Choice Answers

1. b The two variables change in opposite directions.
2. c Pearson correlations are always between 0 and 1, and the sign can be positive or negative.
3. a The larger the correlation (independent of sign), the stronger the relationship.
4. a $r = +0.80$ is a strong positive correlation.
5. c SP $= 74 - 20(30)/10$
6. d The correlation is equal to 4 divided by the square root of (4x16).
7. b Multiplying each X simply shifts the location of the scores. The pattern of the relationship (and the correlation) are not changed.
8. b The table entry for $\alpha = .05$ r $= .396$ and for .01 it is r $= .505$.
9. a The Pearson formula applied to ordinal data produces the Spearman correlation.
10. d The two tied scores are both assigned the average of the tied ranks.
11. c The phi-coefficient is used when both variables are dichotomous.
12. a The slope is fairly large and positive.
13. c $SS_{residual}$ is determined by $1 - r^2$
14. b $2(8) + 3 = 19$
15. b $SS_{residual}$ is determined by $(1 - r^2)SS_Y$

Other Answers

1. For data set I, SP $= 2$. For data set II, SP $= -2$.

2. a. $SS_X = 4$, $SS_Y = 16$, and SP $= 6$. The correlation is r $= 0.75$.
   b. $\hat{Y} = 1.5X + 0.5$

3. The null hypothesis states that there is no relationship in the population. $H_0: \rho = 0$. With n $= 18$, the correlation must be greater than 0.468 to be significant. This sample correlation is not sufficient to conclude that there is a significant correlation in the population.

4. Using Male = 0 and Female = 1, SS = 2, SS = 32, and SP = 4.5 and the point-biserial correlation is r = 0.563.

5. a. The predicted portion is $r^2 = 0.16$ (or 16%)
   b. $SS_{regression} = r^2(SS_Y) = 0.16(90) = 14.4$ with df = 1. $SS_{residual} = (1 - r^2)(SS_Y)$
      $= 0.84(90) = 75.6$ with df = 10. The F-ratio is F = 14.4/7.56 = 1.90. With
      df = 1, 10, this is not significant.

CHAPTER 16

HYPOTHESIS TESTS WITH CHI-SQUARE

CHAPTER SUMMARY

The goals of Chapter 16 are:
1. To introduce the distinction between parametric and nonparametric statistical tests.
2. To demonstrate the chi-square test for goodness of fit.
3. To demonstrate the chi-square test for independence.
4. To demonstrate the measurement of effect size for the test for independence.

Parametric and Nonparametric Tests

Chapter 18 introduces two **non-parametric hypothesis tests** using the chi-square statistic: the chi-square test for goodness of fit and the chi-square test for independence. The term "non-parametric" refers to the fact that the chi-square tests do not require assumptions about population parameters nor do they test hypotheses about population parameters. Previous examples of hypothesis tests, such as the t tests and analysis of variance, are **parametric tests** and they do include assumptions about parameters and hypotheses about parameters. The most obvious difference between the chi-square tests and the other hypothesis tests we have considered (t and ANOVA) is the nature of the data. For chi-square, the data are frequencies rather than numerical scores.

The Chi-Square Test for Goodness-of-Fit

The **chi-square test for goodness-of-fit** uses frequency data from a sample to test hypotheses about the shape or proportions of a population. Each individual in the sample is classified into one category on the scale of measurement. The data, called **observed frequencies**, simply count how many individuals from the sample are in each category. The null hypothesis specifies the proportion of the population that should be in each category. The proportions from the null hypothesis are used to compute **expected frequencies** that describe how the sample would appear if it were in perfect agreement with the null hypothesis.

The Chi-Square Test for Independence

The second chi-square test, the **chi-square test for independence**, can be used and interpreted in two different ways:

1. Testing hypotheses about the relationship between two variables in a population, or
2. Testing hypotheses about differences between proportions for two or more populations.

Although the two versions of the test for independence appear to be different, they are equivalent and they are interchangeable. The first version of the test emphasizes the relationship between chi-square and a correlation, because both procedures examine the relationship between two variables. The second version of the test emphasizes the relationship between chi-square and an independent-measures t test (or ANOVA) because both tests use data from two (or more) samples to test hypotheses about the difference between two (or more) populations.

The first version of the chi-square test for independence views the data as one sample in which each individual is classified on two different variables. The data are usually presented in a matrix with the categories for one variable defining the rows and the categories of the second variable defining the columns. The data, called **observed frequencies**, simply show how many individuals from the sample are in each cell of the matrix. The null hypothesis for this test states that there is no relationship between the two variables; that is, the two variables are independent.

The second version of the test for independence views the data as two (or more) separate samples representing the different populations being compared. The same variable is measured for each sample by classifying individual subjects into categories of the variable. The data are presented in a matrix with the different samples defining the rows and the categories of the variable defining the columns. The data, again called **observed frequencies**, show how many individuals are in each cell of the matrix. The null hypothesis for this test states that the proportions (the distribution across categories) are the same for all of the populations.

Both chi-square tests use the same statistic. The calculation of the chi-square statistic requires two steps:

1. The null hypothesis is used to construct an idealized sample distribution of **expected frequencies** that describes how the sample would look if the data were in perfect agreement with the null hypothesis.

For the goodness of fit test, the expected frequency for each category is obtained by

$$\text{expected frequency} = f_e = pn$$

(p is the proportion from the null hypothesis and n is the size of the sample)

For the test for independence, the expected frequency for each cell in the matrix is obtained by

$$\text{expected frequency} = f_e = \frac{(\text{row total})(\text{column total})}{n}$$

2. A chi-square statistic is computed to measure the amount of discrepancy between the ideal sample (expected frequencies from H_0) and the actual sample data (the observed frequencies = f_o). A large discrepancy results in a large value for chi-square and indicates that the data do not fit the null hypothesis and the hypothesis should be rejected. The calculation of chi-square is the same for all chi-square tests:

$$\text{chi-square} = \chi^2 = \Sigma \frac{(f_o - f_e)^2}{f_e}$$

The fact that chi-square tests do not require scores from an interval or ratio scale makes these tests a valuable alternative to the t tests, ANOVA, or correlation, because they can be used with data measured on a nominal or an ordinal scale.

Measuring Effect Size for the Chi-Square Test for Independence
When both variables in the chi-square test for independence consist of exactly two categories (the data form a 2x2 matrix), it is possible to re-code the categories as 0 and 1 for each variable and then compute a correlation known as a **phi-coefficient** that measures the strength of the relationship. (The phi-coefficient was introduced in Chapter 16.) The value of the phi-coefficient, or the squared value which is equivalent to an r^2, is used to measure the effect size. When there are more than two categories for one (or both) of the variables, then you can measure effect size using a modified version of the phi-coefficient known as **Cramér's V**. The value of V is evaluated much the same as a correlation.

LEARNING OBJECTIVES

1. Recognize the experimental situations where a chi-square test is appropriate.

2. Be able to conduct a chi-square test for goodness of fit to evaluate a hypothesis about the shape of a population frequency distribution.

3. Be able to conduct a chi-square test for independence to evaluate a hypothesis about the relationship between two variables.

4. Be able to measure effect size for the test for independence.

NEW TERMS AND CONCEPTS

The following terms were introduced in this chapter. You should be able to define or describe each term and, where appropriate, describe how each term is related to other terms in the list.

parametric statistical tests

A test evaluating hypotheses about population parameters and making assumptions about parameters. Also, a test requiring numerical scores.

non-parametric statistical tests

A test that does not test hypotheses about parameters or make assumptions about parameters. The data usually consist of frequencies.

expected frequencies

Hypothetical, ideal frequencies that are predicted from the null hypothesis.

observed frequencies

The actual frequencies that are found in the sample data.

chi-square statistic

A test statistic that evaluates the discrepancy between a set of observed frequencies and a set of expected frequencies.

chi-square distribution

The theoretical distribution of chi-square values that would be obtained if the null hypothesis was true.

chi-square test for goodness of fit

A test that uses the proportions found in sample data to test a hypothesis about the corresponding proportions in the general population.

chi-square test for independence

A test that uses the frequencies found in sample data to test a hypothesis about the relationship between two variables in the population.

phi-coefficient

A correlational measure of relationship when both variables consist of exactly two categories. A measure of effect size for the test for independence.

| Cramér's V | A modification of the phi-coefficient to be used when one or both variables consist of more than two categories |

NEW FORMULAS

$$\chi^2 = \Sigma \frac{(f_o - f_e)^2}{f_e}$$

$f_e = pn$ (test for goodness of fit)

$$f_e = \frac{(\text{Row Total})(\text{Column Total})}{n}$$ (test for independence)

$$\text{phi} = \varphi = \frac{\chi^2}{n} \qquad \text{Cramer's V} = \frac{\chi^2}{n(df^*)}$$

where df^* is the smaller of $C - 1$ and $R - 1$.

STEP BY STEP

The chi-square test for independence: The chi-square test for independence uses frequency data to test a hypothesis about the relationship between two variables. The null hypothesis states that the two variables are independent (no relationship). Rejecting H_0 indicates that the data provide convincing evidence of a consistent relationship between the two variables. The following example will be used to demonstrate this chi-square test.

A psychologist would like to examine preferences for the different seasons of the year and how these preferences are related to gender. A sample of 200 people is obtained and the individuals are classified by sex and preference. The psychologist would like to know if there is a consistent relationship between sex and preference. The frequency data are as follows:

	Favorite Season				
	Summer	Fall	Winter	Spring	
Males	28	32	15	45	80
Females	32	8	5	35	120
	60	40	20	80	

Step 1: State the hypotheses and select an alpha level. The null hypothesis says that the two variables are independent.

H_0: Preference is independent of sex. One version of the null hypothesis states that there is no relationship between preference and sex. The second version of H_0 states that there is no difference between the distribution of preferences for males and the distribution of preferences for females (both distributions have the same proportions).

The alternative hypothesis simply says that the two variables are not independent.

H_1: Preference is related to sex, or the distribution of preferences is different for males and females.

We will use $\alpha = .05$

Step 2: Locate the critical region. The degrees of freedom for the chi-square test for independence are
$$df = (C - 1)(R - 1)$$
For this example, $df = 3(1) = 3$. Sketch the distribution and locate the extreme 5%. The critical boundary is 7.81.

The χ^2 distribution with df = 3

Fail to Reject H_0

Reject H_0

0

$\chi^2 = 7.81$

Step 3: Compute the test statistic. The major concern for this chi-square test is determining the expected frequencies. We begin with a blank matrix showing only the row and column totals from the data.

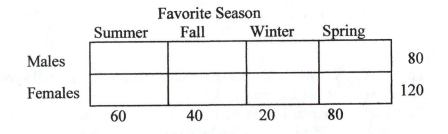

Favorite Season

	Summer	Fall	Winter	Spring	
Males					80
Females					120
	60	40	20	80	

The expected frequencies can be computed using the equation, or they can be determined directly from the null hypothesis. In this example, H_0 says that the distribution of preferences is the same for both genders. Therefore, we must determine the "distribution of preferences."

   For the total sample of n = 200 the data show:
     60/200 = 30% prefer Summer
     40/200 = 20% prefer Fall
     20/200 = 10% prefer Winter
     80/200 = 40% prefer Spring

Next, we apply this distribution to each gender group.

There are 120 males. Using the proportions from the overall distribution, we would expect:
       30% of 120 = 36 males prefer summer
       20% of 120 = 24 males prefer fall
       10% of 120 = 12 males prefer winter
       40% of 120 = 48 males prefer spring

For the group of 80 females we would expect:
       30% of 80 = 24 females prefer summer
       20% of 80 = 16 females prefer fall
       10% of 80 = 8 females prefer winter
       40% of 80 = 32 females prefer spring

Place these values in a matrix of expected frequencies as follows:

Favorite Season

	Summer	Fall	Winter	Spring	
Males	36	24	12	48	80
Females	24	16	8	32	120
	60	40	20	80	

Now you are ready to compute the chi-square statistic.
a) For each cell in the matrix, find the difference between the expected and the observed frequency.
b) Square the difference.
c) Divide the squared difference by the expected frequency.
d) Sum the resulting values for each category

f_o	f_e	$(f_o - f_e)$	$(f_o - f_e)^2$	$(f_o - f_e)^2/f_e$
28	36	-8	64	1.78
32	24	8	64	2.67
15	12	3	9	0.75
45	48	-3	9	0.19
32	24	8	64	2.67
8	16	-8	64	4.00
5	8	-3	9	1.13
35	32	3	9	0.28

$$13.47 = \chi^2$$

Step 4: Make decision. The chi-square value is in the critical region. Therefore, we reject H_0 and conclude hat there is a significant relation between sex and preferred season.

To describe the nature of the relationship, you can compare the data with the expected frequencies. From this comparison it should be clear that more men prefer fall and more women prefer summer than would be expected by chance.

HINTS AND CAUTIONS

1. When computing expected frequencies for either chi-square test, it is wise to check your arithmetic by being certain that $\Sigma f_e = \Sigma f_o = n$. In the test for independence, the expected frequencies in any row or column should sum to the same total as the corresponding row or column in the observed frequencies.

2. Whenever a chi-square test has df = 1, the difference (absolute value) between f_o and f_e will be the same for every category. This is true for either the goodness of fit test with 2 categories, or the test of independence with 4 categories. Knowing this fact can help you check the calculation of expected frequencies and it can simplify the calculation of the chi-square statistic.

SELF TEST

True/False Questions

1. The observed frequencies for a chi-square test represent an ideal, hypothetical distribution that would be obtained if the sample were in perfect agreement with the null hypothesis.

2. In a chi-square test, the observed frequencies are always whole numbers.

3. The value obtained for the chi-square statistic will always be greater than or equal to zero.

4. A researcher uses a chi-square test for goodness of fit to evaluate preferences among four leading brands of ice cream using a sample of 80 people. The chi-square statistic for this test will have df = 79.

5. The null hypothesis for the chi-square test for independence specifies that the proportions in one row of the matrix are identical to the proportions in any other row.

6. The df value for a chi-square test does *not* depend on the sample size.

7. If the null hypothesis for a goodness-of-fit test predicts no preference, then the expected frequencies will be the same for every category.

8. In general, a large value for the chi-square statistic indicates that the null hypothesis is correct.

9. The value obtained for a chi-square statistic tends to increase as the degrees of freedom increase.

10. The phi-coefficient can be used to measure effect size for a chi-square test for independence provided there are exactly two categories for each of the two variables.

Multiple-Choice Questions

1. A characteristic of nonparametric tests is that _____.
   a. they require a numerical score for each individual
   b. they require assumptions about the population distribution(s)
   c. they evaluate hypotheses about population means or variances
   d. None of the other choices is a characteristic of a nonparametric test.

2. The observed frequencies _____.
   a. are always whole numbers
   b. can contain fractions or decimal values
   c. can contain both positive and negative values
   d. can contain fractions and negative numbers

3. Which of the following most accurately describes the expected frequencies in a chi-square test?
   a. They are the frequencies that are found in the sample.
   b. They are sample frequencies that are computed from the null hypothesis.
   c. They are the population frequencies that are specified by the null hypothesis.
   d. They are the population proportions that are specified by the null hypothesis.

4. The chi-square distribution is
   a. symmetrical, centered at a value of zero.
   b. symmetrical, centered at a value determined by the degrees of freedom.
   c. positively skewed, with no values less than zero.
   d. negatively skewed, with no values greater than zero.

5. A researcher hypothesizes that freshmen, sophomores, juniors, and seniors are represented equally among students who volunteer as research participants. The researcher intends to test this hypothesis by selecting a sample of $n = 80$ research volunteers. For the chi-square test, what is the expected frequency for freshmen.

    a. 10
    b. 20
    c. 40
    d. It depends on the proportion of freshmen in the population of students.

6. As the differences between f_e and f_o increase _____.

    a. the likelihood of rejecting H_0 also increases
    b. the likelihood of rejecting H_0 decreases
    c. the critical value for chi-square increases
    d. the critical value for chi-square decreases

7. A researcher is using a chi-square test to determine whether people have any preferences among three brands of televisions. The null hypothesis for this test would state that _____.

    a. there are real preferences in the population
    b. one-third of the sample will prefer each brand
    c. one-third of the population prefers each brand
    d. in the population, one brand is preferred over the other two

8. What does it mean to obtain a large value for the chi-square statistic?

    a. The observed frequencies are large.
    b. The expected frequencies are large.
    c. Both the observed and the expected frequencies are large.
    d. The discrepancy between the observed and expected frequencies is large.

9. A chi-square test for goodness of fit has $df = 2$. How many categories were used to classify the individuals in the sample?

    a. 2
    b. 3
    c. 4
    d. cannot be determined without additional information

10. For a fixed level of significance, the critical value for chi-square will _____.
    a. increase as n increases
    b. decrease as n increases
    c. increase as df increases
    d. decrease as df increases

11. A sample of 100 people is classified by gender (male/female) and by whether or not they are registered voters. The sample consists of 80 females and 20 males, and has a total of 60 registered voters. If these data were used for a chi-square test for independence, the expected frequencies should have a total of _____ males.
    a. 12
    b. 20
    c. 40
    d. 48

12. A sample of 100 people is classified by gender (male/female) and by whether or not they are registered voters. The sample consists of 80 females and 20 males, and has a total of 60 registered voters. If these data were used for a chi-square test for independence, the expected frequencies should have _____ males who are registered voters.
    a. 12
    b. 20
    c. 40
    d. cannot determine without additional information

13. A chi-square test for independence is being used to evaluate the relationship between two variables, one of which is classified into 3 categories and the second of which is classified into 4 categories. The chi-square statistic for this test would have df equal to

_____.
    a. 6
    b. 7
    c. 10
    d. 11

14. A researcher is using a chi-square test to determine whether there are any preferences among four brands of cola. With $\alpha = .05$ and a sample of $n = 30$, what is the boundary for the critical region for the hypothesis test?

    a. 7.81

    b. 9.49

    c. 42.56

    d. 43.77

15. How does sample size influence effect size and the likelihood of significance for the chi-square test for independence?

    a. A larger sample increases both the effect size and the likelihood of significance.

    b. A larger sample increases effect size but does not influence the likelihood of significance.

    c. A larger sample increases the likelihood of significance but does not influence effect size.

    d. A larger sample does not influence either effect size or likelihood of significance.

Other Questions

1. A researcher is examining preferences among four new flavors of ice cream. A sample of $n = 80$ people is obtained. Each person tastes all four flavors and then picks his/her favorite. The distribution of preferences is as follows.

Ice Cream Flavor

A	B	C	D
12	18	28	22

Do these data indicate any significant preferences among the four flavors? Test at the .05 level of significance.

2. A researcher is testing four new flavors of bubble gum using a sample that consists of 50 men, 200 women, and 250 children. Each individual selects his/her favorite flavor. In the total sample of 500 people, 100 selected Flavor A, 200 chose B, 150 picked C, and only 50 preferred D.

    a. If these data are used for a chi-square test for independence, state the null hypothesis.

b. Use the following matrix to fill in the expected frequencies for the chi-square test for independence.

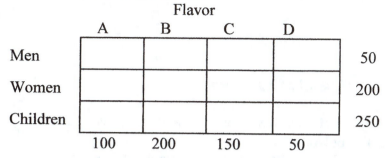

Flavor

	A	B	C	D	
Men					50
Women					200
Children					250
	100	200	150	50	

3. A researcher is interested in the relationship between birth order and personality. A sample of n = 100 people is obtained, all of whom grew up in families as one of three children. Each person is given a personality test and the researcher also records the person's birth order position (1st born, 2nd, or 3rd). The frequencies from this study are shown in the following table. On the basis of these data can the researcher conclude that there is a significant relation between birth order and personality? Test at the .05 level of significance.

Birth Position

	1st	2nd	3rd
Outgoing	13	31	16
Reserved	17	19	4

ANSWERS TO SELF TEST

True/False Answers

1. False The observed frequencies are the values found in the sample data.
2. True
3. True
4. False. For the chi-square tests, degrees of freedom are determined by the number of categories, not the number of subjects. In this case, df = 3.
5. True.
6. True.
7. True
8. False A large value for chi-square indicates that the data do not fit the hypothesis and H_0 should be rejected.

9. True
10. True

Multiple-Choice Answers

1. d Nonparametric tests do not involve parameters and make few if any assumptions about populations.
2. a The observed frequencies are obtained by counting individuals in the sample.
3. b The expected frequencies represent an ideal sample in perfect accord with the null hypothesis.
4. c Chi square is a sum of squared values so it is always positive and the distribution is cut off at zero.
5. b If the four classes are equally represented, then $p = 0.25$ for each. All of the expected frequencies are $0.25(80) = 20$.
6. a The greater the difference between the data and the hypothesis, the greater the likelihood of rejecting the null hypothesis.
7. c Equal preferences implies equal proportions in the population.
8. d The chi-square statistic measures the discrepancy between the data and the null hypothesis.
9. b df = the number of categories minus one for the goodness of fit test.
10. c The chi-square statistic is obtained by adding values across the different categories. the more categories, the larger the value for chi-square.
11. b The column totals and row totals must be the same for the observed frequencies and the expected frequencies.
12. a 60% of 20 males equals 12 males.
13. a $(3 - 1)(4 - 1) = 6$
14. a With $df = 4 - 1 = 3$ and $\alpha = .05$, chi square must be greater than 7.81 to be significant.
15. c As with all tests, sample size influences significance but has little or no effect on measures of effect size.

Other Answers

1. The null hypothesis states that there are no preferences among the four flavors and that 1/4th of the population should prefer each flavor. The expected frequency are 20 for each flavor. With $df = 3$, the critical value is 7.81. For these data, the chi-square statistic is 6.80. The decision is to fail to reject the null hypothesis and conclude that the data do not provide sufficient evidence to indicate significant preferences among the four ice cream flavors.

2. a. One version of the null hypothesis states that gum preference is independent of the age/gender classifications. The second version of H_0 states that the distribution of flavor preferences is the same (same proportions) for men, women, and children.

b.

	Flavor				
	A	B	C	D	
Men	10	20	15	5	50
Women	40	80	60	20	200
Children	50	100	75	25	250
	100	200	150	50	

3. The null hypothesis states that there is no relation between birth order and personality - the two variables are independent. With $df = 2$, the critical value for this test is 5.99. The expected frequencies are as follows:

	Birth Position		
	1st	2nd	3rd
Outgoing	18	30	12
Reserved	12	20	8

For these data, the chi-square statistic is 6.89. Reject H_0 and conclude that there is a significant relation between personality and birth order.